Praise for *14 Fresh*

So, you want to read the Bible but d[o]
want to get more out of your reading
more clearly. This book is for you. Le[t]
you through these simple but effect[...]
Bible. Find the freshness you've been looking for in your [...]
reading *14 Fresh Ways to Enjoy the Bible.*

MICHAEL RYDELNIK
Professor of Jewish Studies and Bible, Moody Bible Institute; syndicated radio
host / Bible teacher on *Open Line with Dr. Michael Rydelnik*

No book in history has had the power to dramatically change the lives and life per-
spectives of its readers than the Bible. So it's no wonder that believers seek to read
it regularly out of respect for its divine author and with the hope of personal profit.
Yet, over time, the exercise of reading the text can have a way of becoming routine
and more of a duty than a delight. So, if you are looking for a way to reinvigorate
your time in the Word, Jim Coakley's insights into the different lenses in which to
see Scripture is just what you are looking for! Highly recommended!

JOE STOWELL
Former President, Moody Bible Institute

We all have our favorite foods, favorite clothes, and favorite songs. But every so
often we need a little change and variety to keep life from becoming too monoto-
nous. And the same is true when we read God's Word. The one-and-done chapter-
a-day approach, or the read-through-the-Bible-in-a-year program are both fine, but
they can also make us focus so intently on "getting through" that we miss the joy
of interacting with the text. Looking for a fresh way to enjoy your time in God's
Word? Then read this book by Dr. James Coakley! Jim provides fourteen new and
exciting ways to enjoy the Bible you likely haven't explored before. These are not
gimmicks or fads. Based on his years of studying and teaching, Jim shares how the
Bible is structured in ways that will help the message become clearer and more
understandable. He also provides biblical examples for each technique to help you
discover for yourself how it helps reveal the meaning of the text. If you want to take
your Bible study to a new level, then read *14 Fresh Ways to Enjoy the Bible.* You will
discover new ways to make your time in God's Word fresh and exciting!

CHARLES DYER
Professor-at-Large of Bible at Moody Bible Institute; host of *The Land and the Book*
radio program

I love this book! It is simply brilliant. James Coakley knows that to understand what
the Bible says, you have to understand how it says it. He knows that the Bible is a literary masterpiece, and he is skilled at helping readers enjoy its literary techniques
(how it says it) as a window into its meaning (what it says). Everything about this
book is fresh—the writing, the ideas, and the examples. Coakley's volume has
helped me become a better Bible reader and has given me a deeper love for God
and His Word.

STEVEN MATHEWSON
Senior Pastor, CrossLife Evangelical Free Church (Libertyville, IL); Director of
the Doctor of Ministry program, Western Seminary (Portland, OR)

Bible readers will want to read this book! Coakley makes all the pro tips from the experts very easy to understand. As a seasoned explorer, excited about new discoveries himself, he shows readers what to look for in the text as we mine the depths of Scripture.

TIM M. SIGLER
Provost & Dean | Professor of Hebrew & Biblical Studies, Shepherds Theological Seminary

It's hard to talk to Jim Coakley without quickly picking up on his love for God's Word and commitment to helping others love it too. In *14 Fresh Ways to Enjoy the Bible*, Jim gives every Christian a tool not just to dig deeper into God's Word but to learn more deeply who God is. As a Bible teacher, I'm always looking for ways to help others better understand their Bibles in order to more deeply love the God who wrote the Bible, and Jim superbly gives us a practical and usable tool to do just that. Get this book, read it, and enjoy its fruit in your life for years to come. You can thank me later.

LINA ABUJAMRA
Founder, Living with Power Ministries; author of *Fractured Faith: Finding Your Way Back to God in an Age of Deconstructions*

As a decades-long literature teacher, I know novels and stories change lives. Why then do sincere Christians, longing to find the Bible interesting, "power through" a text, even great narratives, dutifully, unmoved? This book, treating the Bible as the literary book it is, teaches the reader to see the beauty, design, and cleverness of biblical text. In an utterly engaging, sometimes funny, always approachable manner, Dr. Coakley teaches us how to read well, illustrating with film and literature, classic and contemporary (Tolkien, Forrest Gump, Shakespeare, Steinbeck, etc.). It is a book I will recommend again and again.

ROSALIE DE ROSSET
Professor of literature, Moody Bible Institute

In *14 Fresh Ways to Enjoy the Bible*, James Coakley guides readers in attending to important literary features in the biblical text. The volume avoids technical language, is written in a clear and down-to-earth style, and provides a multitude of examples from both the Bible and nonbiblical works. Students won't even know how much they're learning!

MARK L. STRAUSS
Professor of New Testament at Bethel Seminary of Bethel University and Vice-Chair, NIV Committee on Bible Translation

You're about to take a trip with one of the finest Bible guides I've ever met. *14 Fresh Ways to Enjoy the Bible* is a master class on how to help people see things in the Scriptures that are easily missed. Jim's passion for fresh biblical discovery is contagious, and his illustrations are gripping. You'll find yourself turning the pages of Scripture with a clearer vision of what to look for and eager anticipation of liberating truths to be applied—a truly life-changing book.

KARL CLAUSON
Pastor at 180 Chicago Church, host of *Karl & Crew Mornings*, and author of *The 7 Resolutions: Where Self-Help Ends and God's Power Begins*

14 Fresh Ways to Enjoy the Bible

JAMES F. COAKLEY

MOODY PUBLISHERS

CHICAGO

Edited by Connor Sterchi
Interior design: Erik M. Peterson
Cover design: Darren Welch
Cover illustration of watercolor paper copyright © 2022 by petekarici / Shutterstock (483452421). All rights reserved.

ISBN: 978-0-8024-2885-1

Originally delivered by fleets of horse-drawn wagons, the affordable paperbacks from D. L. Moody's publishing house resourced the church and served everyday people. Now, after more than 125 years of publishing and ministry, Moody Publishers' mission remains the same—even if our delivery systems have changed a bit. For more information on other books (and resources) created from a biblical perspective, go to www.moodypublishers.com or write to:

Moody Publishers
820 N. LaSalle Boulevard
Chicago, IL 60610

3 5 7 9 10 8 6 4 2

Printed in the United States of America

Contents

To all my former professors who instilled in me a deep love for God's Word. To all my former students and small group participants who allowed me to hone the concepts presented in this book. To my present colleagues, friends, and 180 Chicago church family who have provided spiritual, emotional, and intellectual support and stimulation. But most of all to my beloved wife, Gayle, and our two children, Rachel and Joel, for allowing me the privilege of being called husband and father and for all the joy they have brought me, this book is fondly dedicated.

"For My hand made all these things, Thus all these things came into being," declares the LORD. "But to this one I will look, To him who is humble and contrite of spirit, and who trembles at My word." (Isaiah 66:2 NASB)

Introduction

Growing up, a weekly ritual was for our family to sit around the television on a Sunday evening watching classic movies. This was in the 1960s, and for most of that decade our family only had a black-and-white TV. In the middle of that decade, our family was finally able to exchange our black-and-white TV for a Zenith color television in our living room!

This was, of course, long before streaming was available, so you had to watch movies while they were being aired live on a local channel. This was also before large screen TVs, so everyone had to gather close together to view the screen.

One such movie was *The Wizard of Oz*, and it only aired once a year. Since my father was a big Judy Garland fan, it was required viewing for every member of our family. The film starts out in black-and-white with Dorothy and her dog, Toto, in a rural and depressed dust bowl environment. After a tornado whisks Dorothy and her house up into the air in a traumatizing scene, they set down in a faraway land. As Dorothy leaves the house with Toto, the film switches to dazzling color. Dorothy surveys the bright and exotic new surroundings, exclaiming, "Toto, I've a feeling we're not in Kansas anymore."

Hopefully this book has a similar effect. That it will take you on a journey of God's Word. That it will open up your eyes to see new and fresh things about the Bible that will make reading the Scriptures a more enjoyable experience. This book is meant not only to make you marvel as you encounter the creative artistry of God's Word but also to equip you for a lifetime of fresh and delightful discoveries as you put these techniques to use whenever you open the Bible.

The fact that you are reading this book shows that you are sensing a need to take your Bible reading to a new level. Perhaps your time in God's Word has become routine and dull. Hopefully this book will encourage you to freshen your approach to God's Word with easy-to-implement strategies. The Bible is the most read book in all the world, yet sadly it is not often read well. Many get stuck in a rut when approaching the Word. We need practical tools that can revitalize and rejuvenate our reading of Scripture. That's the aim of this book: to equip you with strategies for maximizing your reading pleasure of the Bible.

Many of the techniques described in this book were developed by observing the artful and skillful ways in which authors compose literary texts. Since the Bible is a literary book, it should not be surprising that it contains some of the same devices that great authors implement as they go about their craft. If God has created beauty and structure in the created world around us on both the macro and micro level, it should not surprise us that the same beauty and design is also woven into the revealed Word of God.

The techniques and skills mentioned in this book do not require advanced training. To be sure, learning the biblical languages provides more tools to become better readers of the text, but all you need to apply the principles in this book is a willingness to expand your current reading strategy by implementing new techniques.

Also, when I talk about techniques that the biblical author incorporates into the text of Scripture, I am talking about the intentionality of both the human author and divine author. The human author and divine author worked in harmony. Human authors were divinely moved and inspired by God to write His Word. As 2 Timothy 3:16 reminds us, "All Scripture is inspired by God" (NASB).

Like many Christians, I have had a varied track record when it comes to enjoying reading the Bible. Some days are exhilarating while other days are dull and boring. Throughout my theological education and even while I was a pastor, I was certainly committed to reading it regularly, but I often just powered through it to check it off a daily to-do list. For the most part, I was what you would call a passive Bible reader. I was content to focus on the people, places, and events described in the text without too much attention to how the biblical authors were crafting that information beyond historical accuracy.

How to Read This Book

Let me suggest what might be the best strategy in maximizing your enjoyment as you discover the contents of this book. If you read it from cover to cover in a few sessions, expect to be overwhelmed (hopefully in a good way!) by the sheer number of new insights that perhaps you have never seen before. You will be amazed at the artistry contained within the pages of the Bible and come away dazzled that you have just been in the presence of a literary masterpiece. It is not without reason that the Bible is a revered and respected work, even by many nonbelievers, just based on the sheer brilliance of composition.

Perhaps the best way to benefit from this book is to read a chapter at a time, looking up the passages mentioned by way of example. This way, you can see the technique described in the full context of the biblical author so that it models the way you can implement it in your future reading of God's Word.

Another recommendation is to read this book in community with others. It can easily be adapted as the lesson material for a book club or a home- or church-based small group by taking a chapter or two from this book as a topic for each session. Readers in community can use the chapter titles as labels to quickly identify when group members see one of the techniques in use in a Bible passage (e.g., "Look at the chiasm I saw in this chapter").

Notice the Garnishes

Let me state up front what this book is and isn't intended to do. This is not a book on how to study the Bible (although this book will certainly aid you in doing that properly). There are plenty of great books focused on studying the Bible, such as *Living by the Book*[1] or *Grasping God's Word*.[2] Those resources will give you a step-by-step process on how to apply proper Bible study methods in order to accurately interpret the Scriptures. This book is not intended to supplant those works but supplement them by giving you manageable techniques that anyone can implement to make Bible reading more enjoyable. The chapters in this book are strategies on what you should be on the lookout for as you do your reading.

Everyday, nutritious meals are the types of meals we need to remain healthy. Yet occasionally it's great to go out to a fancy restaurant and enjoy a sumptuous meal prepared by chefs, brought to your table by well-dressed servers on fine dishware. Often those plates will have a sprig of green parsley or other garnish to give the dish a splash of color and enhance the presentation. It heightens the fact that this is a special occasion even though it provides no additional nutritional value to the main dish.

Many Bible readers engage the Scriptures by preparing home-cooked, nutritious spiritual meals that nourish their walk with the Lord. But in this book, I want to also show you how some of those meals you have been enjoying can be enhanced by noticing the garnishes that the biblical authors have added to what they wrote. This will make your mealtime feasting on God's Word a much more delightful experience as you receive not only the needed nutrition that God's Word provides but also the expertise of the biblical authors in how they enhanced the presentation of that meal to make it a five-star restaurant experience.

God's Word is not only a record of His revelation to humanity but also a literary masterpiece. Within its artistic pages there are accounts of intrigue, mystery, and valor. There are also tales of disappointment, abandonment, and brokenness. But its enduring message is one of hope, joy, and resurrection. It's the least boring book in the world! Let's dig in.

First Impressions

SUMMARY: In the "First Impressions" technique, readers identify what the biblical author shares about a character's first words, first actions, and any physical descriptors. This can give the reader an accurate thumbnail portrait of that character's traits (both positively and negatively).

PREVALENCE: By its very nature, this technique is only present in narrative texts. Many major Bible characters demonstrate this technique and some minor characters do as well. It does seem to be more prevalent in the Old Testament but can also be implemented in the four gospels and the book of Acts because they are narrative in style.

INSTRUCTION: Look closely at when major characters (and even some minor characters) are introduced for the first time in the Bible and identify their first words (look for quotation marks), first actions, and (if present) any physical descriptors shared about that person. Then reflect on how those preliminary findings help the reader capture an accurate portrait of that person's character (both positively and negatively), which will be evident the rest of the time they appear in Scripture. These early details often form an accurate first impression that is helpful for the reader.

VALUE/PAYOFF: This technique helps readers gain insight into the lives of biblical figures. Biblical authors had to be selective in sharing details. The details shared about a character were intentionally chosen to portray character traits that will be reflected in their later appearances in Scripture. This technique often reveals not only a character's positive traits but also what will be their Achilles' heel—that is, their besetting flaws.

CHALLENGES: This technique requires that readers be somewhat familiar with the story arc of a character's actions and words. Readers can easily isolate a character's first actions, first words, and any physical descriptors, but may not be able to see how they form an accurate first impression until they can identify future actions that point back to what is communicated up front. Physical descriptors are not always present, so the reader may have to rely on the other two components. There is some degree of subjectivity in determining how first impressions accurately reflect their overall character both positively and negatively. Some characters' first actions and words may be spread out over several chapters, which will require more diligence to identify.

EXAMPLES FROM NONBIBLICAL WORKS:

William Shakespeare, *Hamlet:* The first word out of Horatio's mouth is "Friends." As Hamlet's truest friend, we can observe key characteristics of friendship throughout the book.

William Shakespeare, *The Taming of the Shrew*: Katherina begins with "I." As the "shrew" of the play, readers can begin to sense her self-centered approach to life.

The shark hunter Quint in the film *Jaws*: In a town hall meeting discussing how the community of Amity plans to address the great white shark mauling beachgoers, Quint's first scene is of him sitting down in a relaxed position, scratching his fingernails on a chalkboard in a classroom full of the town's leaders. His first words are "Y'all know me. Know how I earn a livin'. I'll catch this bird for you, but it ain't gonna be easy. Bad fish." His physical appearance (scruffy), his improper use of the English language, and his first actions portray him as an uncouth, prickly, irritating fisherman confident in his abilities. This aptly sets up his character for the rest of the film.

A popular maxim goes like this: "You never get a second chance to make a first impression." First impressions are often etched into the mind and hard to overcome with later interactions. The whole field of marketing seeks to create positive first impressions of their product, candidate, or service. They are hoping for a "halo effect" that generates a positive aura around what or who they are pitching. Whenever someone encounters a new person, quick appraisals are formulated based on that individual's behavior, appearance, and speech, which creates an indelible impression.

In giving my testimony of how I came to faith, I often display my high school ID from senior year. That photo was taken a few months before my conversion. It certainly creates an impression because it captures a number of traits that were true about me at that point in my life. The smile portrays a zest for life and an overall joyful disposition. The bronzed facial suntan and bandana illustrate that I was a bit of a "wild" man who loved the outdoors and traveling to new places (I had just spent that summer backpacking in Colorado and canoeing the boundary waters in northern Minnesota and southern Canada). The long hair shows some of the "rebel" streak that characterized my life at that moment.

When I look at that ID today, I still see some of those same traits present in my life over forty years later! I still have an overall joyful disposition, love traveling, and even though it pains me to admit it, I still have a bit of that rebel nature (although I was always a quiet and friendly rebel, or so I like to tell myself). That visual image accurately captured not only a particular moment in my life (I am still surprised that school officials let me get away with wearing that bandana!) but it also captures a number of traits that have characterized me through my entire life.

So it is with biblical authors. They give readers a literary snapshot, a first impression, that sets the tone for the rest of that character's life.

Now to be sure, some initial impressions may not be accurate and can feed into false stereotypes, such as when the prophet Samuel was to anoint the next king of Israel and saw Eliab, the oldest son of Jesse, and thought him fitting to be the next king. But Eliab's heart was not right for the task (1 Sam. 16:6–7). The priest Eli, based on his initial exposure to Hannah, thought that she was drunk when in fact she was extremely pious (1 Sam. 1:8–16). Saul was described as handsome and tall (1 Sam. 9:2), and since those are his only traits listed in the text, it appears that the people thought that his stature and looks would make him an ideal candidate to be king of Israel. That certainly did not turn out to be the case as Saul demonstrated over and over again his inability to properly lead the nation of Israel throughout his reign.

All three of these examples from 1 Samuel—which show that initial impressions may not be accurate—are intentionally included in the book to highlight one of its themes: that outward appearances can be deceiving. The author of 1 Samuel is utilizing the "First Impressions" technique to make a practical application point—we, too, should not rely on outward appearances as a gauge to determine someone's spiritual vitality and character.

With that in mind, it is reasonable to assume that those initial actions, words, and physical descriptors are, more often than not, truly reflective of that individual and their overall character. Authors cannot share everything about an individual, but they can be intentional and selective about what they do share in order to create an accurate portrait of a character's persona in the text.

The way that authors portray individuals is part of what is called "characterization." Authors can use direct methods of portraying a character by stating it plainly, such as when John calls Judas a "thief" (John 12:5–6). Another way that authors help readers develop a better sense of what a character is like is through what is called "indirect characterization," which is when they use roundabout ways of developing a person's character by letting readers externally "see" their early actions or "hear" the first words that come out of their mouth. This subtly reveals internal motivations or character traits.

Of course, the first words uttered from a character in Scripture are not their *actual* first words but the first words we as readers encounter in the text. It often turns out that the information gleaned from this up-front content sets the tone for how this character is going to act in the rest of the narrative.

BIBLICAL EXAMPLES OF "FIRST IMPRESSIONS"

Esau

Let's look at how this plays out in the story of Esau. When Esau is introduced in Genesis 25, here is what Moses communicates about his first actions, first words, and physical description:

FIRST ACTIONS: He is portrayed as a skillful hunter and an outdoorsman (Gen. 25:27).

FIRST WORDS: "Let me eat some of that red stew" (Gen. 25:30).

PHYSICAL DESCRIPTORS: red and hairy (Gen. 25:25)

Keep in mind that this content was intentionally selected out of many things that could have been used to describe Esau. If we take this information and reflect on how it develops Esau as a character, several traits come to the surface that paint a portrait of Esau.

For instance, the fact that he is described as red and hairy (so hairy, in fact, that Jacob later clothes himself in goat skin to mimic his brother when he steals his blessing!) not only explains why he is such an effective hunter (because of his camouflage from all this hair) but also subtly foreshadows his more brutish, animal-like nature as someone who prefers to live in the wild.

In addition, his first words—the churlish way in which he asks for something to eat—show that his stomach is his main motivator.

These details clearly portray Esau in animal-like fashion. Like an animal, he wants instant gratification, and he shows no capacity to understand the long-term benefits of keeping his birthright. Esau looks animal-like, spends a lot of time in open fields like an animal, and brutishly talks like we envision an animal would communicate. This first impression of Esau accurately gives the reader a portrait of his overall general character traits that define the way we encounter him in later texts.

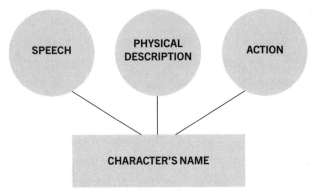

Components of Indirect Characterization

Abraham

FIRST ACTIONS: "Abram went forth as the Lord had spoken to him" and set out for Canaan. When a severe famine struck, he went to Egypt (Gen. 12:4–5, 10 NASB).

FIRST WORDS: "When he was about to enter Egypt, he said to Sarai his wife, 'I know that you are a woman beautiful in appearance, and when the Egyptians see you, they will say, "This is his wife." Then they will kill me, but they will let you live. *Say you are my sister*, that it may go well with me because of you, and that my life may be spared for your sake'" (Gen. 12:11–13).

PHYSICAL DESCRIPTORS: none communicated other than his age (seventy-five) when he set out for Canaan (Gen. 12:4).

Abram's first actions (positively) reveal him to be obedient to God's commands but also (negatively) show his tendency to take matters into his own hands, which he demonstrates by going to Egypt to avoid a famine. This move seems to have been taken unilaterally without consulting God or waiting upon Him to provide. His first recorded speech also reveals this tendency toward expedience and to manipulate situations to his own liking when he tells Sarai to say she is his sister instead of his wife. This combination of sometimes obeying God (as when he is willing to offer up Isaac as a burnt sacrifice in Genesis 22) and sometimes choosing the path of expedience (e.g., in Genesis 12, in bringing his nephew Lot with him from Haran as someone who could take care of him and his estate in case God's promise of a seed did not come through, or choosing to sleep with Hagar to raise up a male heir apart from Sarah in Genesis 16) is a fitting snapshot of Abraham and his walk with God.

Moses

FIRST ACTIONS: "One day, when Moses had grown up, he went out to his people and *looked on their burdens,* and he saw an Egyptian beating a Hebrew, one of his people. *He looked this way and that,* and seeing no one, *he struck down the Egyptian* and hid him in the sand" (Ex. 2:11–12).

FIRST WORDS: "When he went out the next day, behold, two Hebrews were struggling together. And he said to the man in the wrong, '*Why do you strike your companion?*'" (Ex. 2:13).

PHYSICAL DESCRIPTORS: He was a "fine child" (Ex. 2:2). (In this case, it probably means that he was a quiet baby so that his mother could keep him undetected by others.)

Moses' first actions show his compassionate side (he is concerned about his people's burdens) but also his difficulty in controlling his anger. His first words reveal that he seeks justice when he sees unjust actions. So, in summary, what this first impression reveals about Moses is that he is a justice-oriented, compassionate individual who looks out for the underdogs. He also reveals these same traits when he arrives in Midian (see Ex. 2:17) and continues to exemplify them throughout his life. As a result, he is the perfect representative to mediate God's laws to the people. Yet this first impression of him also reveals a negative trait of anger, which will resurface throughout his life, including the incident near the end of the wilderness journey where, instead of speaking to the rock to bring forth water for the people, he strikes the rock twice in anger (Num. 20:10–11). This early information is a fitting snapshot of Moses and his overall character qualities (both positive and negative).

David

FIRST ACTIONS: 1 Samuel 16–17 portrays David doing a number of actions, such as being obedient to his father, Jesse, shepherding the family's flocks, playing the harp in King Saul's court, and fighting Goliath as a warrior in the Valley of Elah.

FIRST WORDS: "And David said to the men who stood by him, 'What shall be done for the man who kills this Philistine and takes away the reproach from Israel? For who is this uncircumcised Philistine, that he should defy the armies of the living God?'" (1 Sam. 17:26).

PHYSICAL DESCRIPTORS: He was the youngest of Jesse's sons, and was "ruddy and had beautiful eyes and was handsome" (1 Sam. 16:11–12).

David is often labeled as a "man after God's own heart" (1 Sam. 13:14), which is expressly demonstrated by his first recorded words. His early recorded actions reveal him to be a shepherd (an apt metaphor for his later leadership skills), a musician (which is fitting since he is a major contributor to the book of Psalms), and a warrior whose military skills will become more evident as the narrative proceeds.

These first actions plant the seeds for the three major roles David will have throughout his life (leader, musician, and warrior). These major character traits are intentionally introduced up front in the narrative. Although embedded with this first impression are David's many positive traits, there is also an introduction to a major character flaw in that he is somewhat self-interested as well. This is revealed by his own lips in the very first words we hear from him when he inquires about what the reward will be for killing Goliath. This focus on "what's in it for him" later reveals itself when he took a census of his own people and committed adultery with Bathsheba.

Like most of us, he is a mixed bag—a man after God's heart, but he can also pursue his own heart and interests as well. David's physical attributes, especially his attractive outer appearance, add tension to the overall account of David's life in that the Bible often depicts attractive people as experiencing more difficulties (Sarah, Rachel, Joseph, Bathsheba, Absalom, etc.).

In summary, the "First Impressions" technique is an easy way to increase the "wow" factor as you read your Bible. You are now able to detect how the biblical authors identify key positive and negative traits of Bible characters by reflecting on a character's first words, first actions, and any physical descriptors. By focusing on these details, readers can not only increase their enjoyment but also gain an inside track into properly assessing an individual's character by seeing how these early actions and speeches paint an accurate first impression that is further depicted later in the narrative.

GO and IMPLEMENT

This technique can be properly utilized with other characters such as Rachel, Sarah, Jacob, Gideon, Samson, Samuel, Saul, Daniel, and John the Baptist. It can also be used in the first two chapters of Genesis by looking at "God's" actions and speech in Genesis 1 and then contrasting and comparing those actions and speech to the "LORD God's" actions and speech in Genesis 2. This reveals great insights into God's character traits by looking at His first actions and words.

FOR FURTHER STUDY

Alter, R. *The Art of Biblical Narrative*. 2nd ed. New York: Basic Books, 2011. (Chapters 4 and 6)

Berlin, A. *Poetics and Interpretation of Biblical Narrative*. Sheffield, UK: The Almond Press, 1983. (pp. 34–37)

Bodner, Keith. *David Observed: A King in the Eyes of His Court*. Sheffield, UK: Sheffield Phoenix Press, 2008. (pp. 17–24)

Gunn, David M., and Danna N. Fewell. *Narrative in the Hebrew Bible*. Oxford: Oxford University Press, 1993. (Chapter 3)

Johnson, Benjamin J. M. "Making a First Impression: The Characterisation of David and His Opening Words in 1 Samuel 17:25–31." *Tyndale Bulletin* 71, no. 1 (2020): 75–93.

Skinner, Christopher W. *Characters and Characterization in the Gospel of John.* London: T&T Clark, 2013. (p. 13)

Walsh, Jerome T. *Old Testament Narrative: A Guide to Interpretation.* Louisville: Westminster John Knox Press, 2009. (Chapter 7)

2

Read the Labels

SUMMARY: "Read the Labels" involves identifying and tracking the various ways that a biblical author references the characters within the book. This allows readers to view the individuals within the account in the way the author intended, or to gain insight into how characters view each other within the account.

PREVALENCE: This is mainly found in narrative texts but also can be used in other genres such as poetry and epistles.

INSTRUCTION: Look for how the biblical author references individuals within the text or how characters label each other within the text and track their usage. Look for patterns, such as whether familial labels are used (husband, sister, son, uncle, etc.), ethnic labels are mentioned (Egyptian, Hittite, Ammonite, etc.), proper names are foregrounded or suppressed, pronouns are used instead of other labels, self-effacing labels such as "your servant" are used, or place of origin is mentioned

(Saul of Tarsus or Joseph of Arimathea). Once the findings are gathered, consider what might have motivated the author to use those particular labels.

VALUE/PAYOFF: Identifying and tracking the labels can help readers detect what the biblical author is foregrounding by way of characterization, rhetorical devices that aid in thematic understanding of the text, or a key viewpoint shift that the narrator wants readers to experience.

CHALLENGES: The only real challenge is that readers must be able to take the information learned in this technique and reflect on why the author chose the particular labels that are used (compared to other labels that could have been used). Authors do not spell out explicitly why these particular labels are used, so there will be some degree of subjectivity in determining the "so what?"

EXAMPLES FROM NONBIBLICAL WORKS:

Indiana Jones and the Last Crusade: Sometimes the main character is called "Junior" by his father to belittle him.

Gladiator: The lead protagonist is named "Maximus"—a fitting name for a warrior. In addition, the character lists all of his labels in a famous line from the film while addressing the crowd in the arena: "My name is Maximus Decimus Meridius, commander of the Armies of the North, General of the Felix Legions, loyal servant to the true emperor, Marcus Aurelius. Father to a murdered son, husband to a murdered wife. And I will have my vengeance, in this life or the next."

Labels on food products are helpful to the consumer because they clearly identify the product so that the purchaser can make an informed decision whether or not to buy the product. In the same way, authors use "labels" when referencing characters within their work. The technical name for this is "participant reference," which considers the choices authors make for referring to characters within the narrative. For instance, I have many "labels," such as Jim, James, husband, father, grandfather, Dr. Coakley, professor, pastor, elder, etc. Some of those labels are formal (Dr. Coakley), some are familial (husband, grandfather), some are related to what I do (professor, elder), and some are only used by those who have a close relationship with me (Jimbo, Dr. C).

All of these labels refer to me, but individually they communicate a certain attribute about me in various contexts and settings. Some labels are out of place in certain settings. For instance, what student would register for a class in an esteemed institution of higher learning if the professor's name was Jimbo?

The "Read the Labels" technique is an easy way to freshen up our Bible reading. While reading, identify and track the labels that an author uses for characters in the story. Once a character is introduced, many Bible readers create a picture in their mind of who that character is and default to that initial picture without looking at the nuanced ways that the author is presenting that character. Identifying and tracking these character labels gives readers an inside look on how the author is wanting to portray a certain facet of that character. It may be familial (David, son of Jesse) or occupational (Simon the tanner). It may show

how characters are viewing other characters within the narrative, whether positively (e.g., when Boaz calls Ruth a "worthy woman") or negatively (e.g., in 1 Samuel 25:25, when Abigail references her husband by his proper name, attaching a negative label: "Let not my lord regard this worthless fellow, Nabal," which means "fool").

Also, pay attention to when pronouns are used instead of proper nouns. Pronouns are typically used to make sentences less repetitive by eliminating the need to repeat the same nouns over and over, but sometimes biblical authors use pronouns instead of proper nouns to add a hint of secrecy to dramatic scenes. For instance, in the threshing room incident in Ruth 3 there appears to be the avoidance of the proper names Ruth and Boaz by the narrator after 3:7, because that enhances the clandestine nature of the encounter that Boaz himself knows could be problematic, since he states in 3:14, "Let it not be known that the woman came to the threshing floor."

In some instances, biblical authors may use pronouns to add ambiguity to the account to force readers to slow down and try to ascertain which referent that the pronoun refers to. One example is Ruth 2:20, when Naomi exclaims to Ruth: "May he be blessed of the LORD who has not withdrawn *his* kindness to the living and to the dead" (NASB). It is not entirely clear to whom the pronoun "his" refers to in this verse: Is it Boaz or the LORD? Evidence could be garnered to support either individual as the referent, and the reader is forced to take time and expend mental effort in trying to figure it out, which may actually be the author's intent. Other examples where biblical authors may have injected ambiguity to cause readers to ponder are 1 Kings 3:16–28 and 20:35–43.

In contrast, look for when proper nouns are repeated multiple times even though pronouns would be adequate. In Genesis 50, Joseph's proper name is repeated seven times in verses 22–26, which is the last paragraph in the book. The repeated use of his personal name at the end of the book not only keeps him in focus in the minds of the readers in his last days on earth but also helps to highlight his personal faith in wanting to be included in the land promise given to his forefathers in Genesis 50:24–25. Abel is referred to as "brother" seven times in Genesis 4, even though that information is already known to readers. Its repeated use emphasizes that Cain is indeed his "brother's keeper," an implicit answer to Cain's sarcastic question: "Am I my brother's keeper?" (Gen. 4:9).

BIBLICAL EXAMPLES OF "READ THE LABELS"

Bathsheba

Here is the text containing the account of David and Bathsheba with all the referents to Bathsheba in bold:

> Then it happened in the spring, at the time when kings go out to battle, that David sent Joab and his servants with him and all Israel, and they destroyed the sons of Ammon and besieged Rabbah. But David stayed at Jerusalem. Now when evening came David arose from his bed and walked around on the roof of the king's house, and from the roof he saw

a woman bathing; and **the woman** was very beautiful in appearance. So David sent and inquired about **the woman**. And one said, "Is this not **Bathsheba, the daughter of Eliam, the wife of Uriah the Hittite?**" David sent messengers and took **her**, and when **she** came to him, he lay with **her**; and when **she** had purified herself from **her** uncleanness, **she** returned to **her** house. The woman conceived; and **she** sent and told David, and said, "I am pregnant." (2 Sam. 11:1–5 NASB)

Several observations can now be made tracking all the references to Bathsheba:

1) The author portrays David as objectifying her first by referring to her as just a "woman." This is seen by focusing on her gender and not any other label that would elevate her personal identity and status. (Samson does the same thing in Judges 14:1–3.)

2) An unnamed court official stated her true identity with her proper name and family identity: "Bathsheba, the daughter of Eliam, the wife of Uriah the Hittite." All of this information should have given David pause in pursuing her.

3) The narrator of the account shows her with little control over her situation by simply using pronouns (*her, she*) instead of her proper name (Bathsheba). This adds to the clandestine nature of the scene in general and clearly makes David the aggressor in this act of adultery.

Ishmael

In Genesis 17:18–26, Ishmael's personal name and status are clearly mentioned. However, in Genesis 21:9–15, there are eighteen references to Ishmael as a character, but his personal name is never used by anyone. Instead, he is referred to with more impersonal labels such as *lad, boy, son of Hagar the Egyptian, son of the maid,* and *her son.* Readers should sense this marginalizing of Ishmael by tracking the use of the labels used to reference him. This fits the author's intent by having Ishmael leave the narrative stage so that readers focus on the child of promise, Isaac.

Ruth

Tracking the labels used for Ruth gives readers insight into properly understanding how others viewed her.

- **Narrator:** uses a wide array of labels. The author of Ruth intentionally uses the label "Ruth the Moabitess" in Ruth 1:22, even though the reader clearly understands her Moabite ancestry. This repetition raises the tension in the account by highlighting that an Israelite from the tribe of Judah is coming home to Bethlehem with a hated Moabite. In Ruth 2:2, the narrator once again uses the label "Ruth the Moabitess" to stress the dire straits of Naomi's and Ruth's predicament—it is challenging enough for a local resident to forage for food in the community but even more difficult for a foreign woman (and a Moabite one at that) to do so.

- **Naomi:** repeatedly references Ruth as "daughter," stressing her familial maternal role.

- **Ruth:** self-references herself as "foreigner," "maidservant," and "your maid," clearly showing her to be deferential and unassertive.

- **Boaz:** When speaking to Ruth directly, he calls her "daughter" (signaling a significant age gap between him and her) and "worthy woman" (which demonstrates that he holds her in high regard). Interestingly, when he references her to the closer relative in Ruth 4:5, he plays the race card for his advantage when he states that "you must also acquire Ruth the Moabitess," as if mentioning her ethnicity will cause the closer relative to think twice about redeeming Naomi's property. In almost comical fashion, he adds that she is the "widow of the deceased" to make her even less appealing (i.e., "Are you sure you want to marry someone whose first husband died?"). Boaz, however, later in the account proclaims that "I have acquired Ruth the Moabitess, the widow of Mahlon to be my wife" (4:10), demonstrating that her ethnicity and marital history are not hurdles for him.

Here are a few general observations about this technique to be on the lookout for:

1) Negative assessments are generally the rule when characters are:
   - referred to by ethnic titles (Aramean, Edomite, Philistine, etc.).
   - referred to as the "son of" due to stressing the diminutive relationship or because it is used pejoratively "son

of Mary" (Mark 6:3) [major exception with the phrase "Son of God"].

- combined with "that/this" demonstrative pronoun— e.g., "this Philistine" (1 Sam. 17:26).
- labeled with some occupation, such as "the carpenter" (Mark 6:3), or "Simon the tanner" (Acts 10:6). However, one would expect the label "Rahab the harlot" to be entirely negative, but that label is used by New Testament writers to highlight God's transforming grace in her life (Heb. 11:31; James 2:25).
- showing deference in the accounts when they avoid first-person pronouns—e.g., "your servant" (1 Sam. 20:7–8).

2) Notice characters who do not possess a personal name. They are typically defined by nouns indicating their occupation or title (e.g., the "shield-bearer" in 1 Samuel 17:7). Usually, anonymous figures carry a negative stigma (e.g., witch of Endor) or identify someone without any significant social standing (e.g., Abraham's two young servants in Genesis 22:3–5), but sometimes the lack of a proper name forces the reader to slow down and ponder why these anonymous figures are present in the narrative and reflect on the reason why the biblical author intentionally left them nameless. It might be to focus on how their occupation plays a significant role as compared to the named characters (e.g., messengers or shield-bearers) or to signal a sense of foreboding (e.g., Jephthah's daughter).

3) Sometimes proper names are suppressed until a pivotal moment, as in the case of David, who is not mentioned by

name in 1 Samuel until after he is anointed and the Spirit of the Lord comes upon him (1 Sam. 17:13).

Tracking all the labels that are applied to the characters you come across in your Bible reading is a simple but surefire way to energize and enliven the time you spend in God's Word. Plus, it will provide you with something to direct the focus of your reading that can lead to delightful personal observations.

GO and IMPLEMENT

GENESIS 4: Try this on your own with Abel in Genesis 4. Take note of how often his proper name is mentioned and then reflect on its absence in verses 10–11.

GENESIS 28–31: Track the character Laban by the labels he possesses in Genesis 28–30 and then notice the shift in how he is referred as in Genesis 31:20–24.

THE GOSPELS: As you read through one of the Gospels, see all the "labels" that characters within the book use when addressing Jesus (e.g., master, rabbi, teacher, Lord, etc.) and look for how those titles give insight into how those characters view Jesus.

FOR FURTHER STUDY

Chirichigno, Gregory. "The Use of the Epithet in the Characterization of Joshua." *Trinity Journal* 8, no. 1 (1987): 69–79.

Chun, S. Min. *Ethics and Biblical Narrative: A Literary and Discourse-Analytical Approach to the Story of Josiah.* Oxford: Oxford University Press, 2014. (pp. 133–35)

Reinhartz, Adele. *"Why Ask My Name?": Anonymity and Identity in Biblical Narrative.* New York: Oxford University Press, 1998.

Vreeland, Gerald D. *The Darker Side of Samuel, Saul and David: Narrative Artistry and the Depiction of Flawed Leadership,* vol. 1. Maitland, FL: Xulon Press, 2007. (pp. 375–77)

Wenger, Rachelle. "Redundancy Is Information: The Literary Function of Participant Reference in Biblical Hebrew Narrative." *The Bible Translator* 63, no. 4 (2012): 179–84.

3

Step Up to the Mic

SUMMARY: This technique calls on readers to isolate direct speech and contemplate how they not only reveal the speaker's character but also how they often convey key theological and thematic points that the author intends readers to identify.

PREVALENCE: Extensively used in narrative texts but also present in other genres of the Bible.

INSTRUCTION: Look for quotation marks and isolate the direct speech that characters make. Reflect on how those words either reveal a character trait or express a main theological or literary theme of the passage.

VALUE/PAYOFF: This technique is one of the quickest ways for readers to ascertain what truly motivates a character. In addition, a character often voices key themes of the passage that the author is highlighting, so it can be used as a means to determine whether a reader is tracking what the biblical author is intending to convey.

CHALLENGES: This technique is easiest to identify when the biblical author inserts a single direct speech quote from the lips of one of the characters as compared to a text with extended back-and-forth dialogue between two parties. It is also a lot harder to analyze longer speeches, such as the Sermon on the Mount (Matt. 5–7) or Stephen's speech (Acts 7), since they are extended discourses, making it harder to isolate foregrounded statements.

EXAMPLES FROM NONBIBLICAL WORKS:

Shawshank Redemption (1994 film): Andy Dufresne's conversation with his friend Red not only forecasts Andy's future plans to live in Mexico but also captures one of the main themes: "I guess it comes down to a simple choice really: get busy living or get busy dying." It is a story about the human struggle to overcome adversity and move beyond whatever obstacles are in our way to realize our dreams and aspirations. Andy overcame twenty years of false imprisonment, never giving up hope, working patiently until he was able to escape.

Independence Day (1996 film): President Thomas Whitmore addresses a ragtag unit before a battle that will determine the fate of all mankind and states: "Mankind—that word should have new meaning for all of us today. We can't be consumed by our petty differences anymore. We will be united in our common interests. Perhaps it's fate that today is the 4th of July, and you will once again be fighting for our freedom, not from tyranny, oppression, or persecution—but from annihilation."

This speech sets up the theme that people, working together despite their differences, can overcome great odds and protect humanity.

As humans we have countless conversations, but on occasion some spoken words have more impact than others. Conversations with a checkout clerk at a store counter are routine and for the most part forgettable, but if you are in a doctor's office discussing recent lab test results, you would hang on every word that the physician says in order to get their expert opinion of your condition and prognosis.

I have sat on a jury several times throughout my life. Lawyers on both sides of a case tried to influence the jury to agree with their presentation of the evidence, but when the principal litigants were called to the witness stand, I tended to be much more alert to their exact words stated on the stand, since the case was centered on them, and their oral testimony carried more weight. Biblical authors are like courtroom lawyers in that they present a literary case for readers, but sometimes they allow for the characters to address the reader in their own words, often for thematic purposes.

English Bible translations make finding these "Step Up to the Mic" occurrences easy to spot because of quotation marks. Once quotation marks are located, the next step is to ask this question:

"Why is it that the author yielded the microphone to allow us to hear a character speak in their words instead of simply narrating the event?" Many Scripture readers are already aware of the importance of this because of red-letter editions to emphasize the words of Christ. To be sure, these versions may give the subtle message that the words in red are more important than the other words recorded in the gospel accounts, which is not always the case, but it does help in identifying the quoted words of Jesus.

Consider Genesis 12:10–13:

Now there was a famine in the land. So Abram went down to Egypt to sojourn there, for the famine was severe in the land. When he was about to enter Egypt, he said to Sarai his wife, "I know that you are a woman beautiful in appearance, and when the Egyptians see you, they will say, 'This is his wife.' Then they will kill me, but they will let you live. Say you are my sister, that it may go well with me because of you, and that my life may be spared for your sake."

The narrator could have just told us that Abram lied, but instead, we as readers witness Abram lie with his own words. Why did the author allow us to hear the character's words instead of the author summarizing the speech?

Direct speech can accomplish different things that narration is unable to do. It slows down the tempo of the action to zero in on a particular scene where the author wants to stress something. In addition, direct speech often confirms a literary or theological theme that is communicated in the surrounding narrative. When this happens, we hear that theme directly from the lips of the character rather than indirectly from the narrator.

Another benefit of direct speech is that when there is dialogue between two characters, it is an indicator of the type of relationship that exists between them. Is there a power differential? Is there respect and admiration?

When we look for quotation marks and consider why the author gave us the actual words expressed, it helps us to get a more intimate portrait of the character who is speaking. Luke 6:45 gives us this principle succinctly: "The good person out of the good treasure of his heart produces good, and the evil person out of his evil treasure produces evil, for out of the abundance of the heart his mouth speaks."

Biblical authors often "show rather than tell" in narratives. They allow the reader to come to their own conclusion about the rightness or wrongness of a character's actions or words without commentary to that effect. In the case of Abram, the author (Moses) provides us with Abram's own speech to his wife exactly as he said it. Abram then is seen to really "own" this because we are hearing it "straight from the horse's mouth" and not through an intermediary.

This technique is a great way to develop a deeper sense of the speaker's character, and, in many cases, the thrust of the passage is often found on the lips of one of the characters within the story rather than by the narrator recounting the events.

BIBLICAL EXAMPLES OF "STEP UP TO THE MIC"

Genesis 18

Let's look at an example from the life of Abraham. After God announces that He is going to destroy Sodom, Abraham stood before the Lord and said:

"Will you indeed sweep away the righteous with the wicked? Suppose there are fifty righteous within the city. Will you then sweep away the place and not spare it for the fifty righteous who are in it? Far be it from you to do such a thing, to put the righteous to death with the wicked, so that the righteous fare as the wicked! Far be that from you! *Shall not the Judge of all the earth do what is just?*" (Gen. 18:23–25)

This direct speech certainly reveals that Abraham is a compassionate uncle concerned about the well-being of his nephew Lot, who lives in Sodom. In addition, it also summarizes a key theological point about the character of God because Abraham appeals to the just nature of God, which is a theme in the book of Genesis in the face of sin and disobedience.

Luke 23

Another example of this technique is found in Luke's gospel at the crucifixion of Jesus. After Jesus breathed His last breath, a Roman centurion who witnessed what had happened praised God and said, "Surely this was a righteous man" (Luke 23:47).

The author (Luke) intentionally chose to include the centurion's exact statement, not only because it reveals this soldier's character as one who is willing to praise God even though he has a pagan background but also because this centurion (a Gentile outsider) is the first person who gets it, even before any of the disciples do! Luke desires that we, the readers of his gospel account of Jesus' life, will now come to the same fork in the road as this centurion and declare the Son of God to be a righteous man. The only fitting response then for us as readers is to come to the same conclusion that this Roman soldier did.

One way to increase your personal delight in God's Word is to use your "ears" and "mouth" while you are reading with your "eyes." Visualize the account as a scene, and when a character speaks, assign a unique voice to that character so you are able to track when the narrator yields up the microphone and hands it to one of the characters.

GO and IMPLEMENT

GENESIS 22:5–8: Look for evidence from Abraham's own lips of his faith, but also how his direct speeches reveal the big idea of the account in his own words.

GENESIS 39: Carefully investigate the direct speeches of Potiphar's wife and how even the subtle changes in her two spoken alibis (one to the servants of the household and another to her husband) reveal her wicked character, but also how she is willing to use racial animus to get a desired outcome.

EXODUS 1: Identify the speech of the midwives and how it captures a major theme of the book.

FOR FURTHER STUDY

Alter, Robert. *The Art of Biblical Narrative.* 2nd ed. New York: Basic Books, 2011. (Chapter 4)

Berlin, Adele. *Poetics and Interpretation of Biblical Narrative.* Sheffield, UK: The Almond Press, 1983. (pp. 64–72)

Fee, Gordon D., and Douglas K. Stuart. *How to Read the Bible for All Its Worth.* 4th ed. Grand Rapids: Zondervan, 2014. (pp. 100–101)

La Breche, Pamela. "A Methodology for the Analysis of Characterization in Old Testament Narrative." ThM Thesis, Dallas Theological Seminary, 1992. (pp. 33–44)

4

Launching Pad

SUMMARY: This technique involves looking closely at the content at the beginning of a Bible book, which sets the trajectory for the themes of the entire book. Just like rockets heading to space need a solid starting point to complete the mission's objective, the beginning of a book propels the reader in the accurate direction for the journey ahead. The "Launching Pad" base of information serves as a sort of "table of contents" for what will be unpacked in further detail later in the book. This technique is a literary rhetorical device in which the author intentionally selects content to front-load at the beginning of the book, which serves as a primer for content that will be further developed later on.[3]

PREVALENCE: Even though it is not present in every book of the Bible, its presence is commonplace enough to warrant looking for it because it is not limited to a specific genre or Testament.

INSTRUCTION: Focus on the content of the first chapters of a Bible book and then, as you read later chapters, look for how that early material helped set the table thematically for what followed. Once the entire book is read (and ideally reread multiple times), take time to reflect on how that up-front content prepares readers (similar to a table of contents in modern books) by signaling themes that the author wants the reader to focus on.

VALUE/PAYOFF: Structurally, it sets the thematic tone for what the reader is going to encounter later in the book. Practically, it underscores themes that the author wants the reader to ponder as they read, and even after they finish the book. This way the reader has more confidence that they are picking up on the themes that they should be identifying by following those early "breadcrumbs."

CHALLENGES: There will be varying degrees of certainty and subjectivity as to what the intent and value of the "Launching Pad" material may be for the reader. When reading a biblical book with this technique, readers will not usually be able to detect those themes on their first reading, so it does require repeatedly reading the entire book.

EXAMPLES FROM NONBIBLICAL WORKS:
The Lion King: The opening scene—when the animals gather at Pride Rock and are introduced to Simba—sets up the film even without any of the characters speaking a word. Other Disney movies like *Beauty and the Beast* and *Up* have similar opening thematic scenes.

Back to the Future: The opening scene features a number of images that set up major themes of the film, such as a series of clocks (time travel), plutonium, a knob labeled "Overdrive," and a close relationship between Marty and the eccentric Doc. (*Raiders of the Lost Ark* is another example.)

Pride and Prejudice (eighteenth-century novel by Jane Austen): The opening line is "It is a truth universally acknowledged, that a single man in possession of a good fortune must be in want of a wife. However little known the feelings or views of such a man may be on his first entering a neighbourhood, this truth is so well fixed in the minds of the surrounding families, that he is considered as the rightful property of some one or other of their daughters."[4] This points directly to the story of domestic unhappiness and happiness that permeates the rest of the book.

1984 (novel written by George Orwell in 1949): The book's opening line sets up this dystopian novel by introducing the theme that nothing is certain or fixed: "It was a bright cold day in April, and the clocks were striking thirteen."[5] Time itself has been disoriented when a government excises God.

Communicators know the value of the statement often attributed to Aristotle in book five of his work *Politics*, "Well begun is half done."[6] In modern writing, it is critical to begin well if an author wants to draw the reader in. It is also just as important to introduce the topic or theme as soon as possible so that the reader has some notion of what the author is seeking to accomplish. As a professor I grade a lot of students' papers. One of the first things I look for in the introduction is a thesis statement where the student clearly defines what the paper is all about. Papers without such a statement tend to meander because there is not an overarching theme unifying the individual paragraphs in the body of the submitted assignment.

The challenge for Scripture reading is that the biblical authors do not use what modern-day readers are accustomed to in the introductions of their books. When we look at a book today, we have many ways to help us ascertain what the book is about: the book's title, the back cover, and the table of contents can all reveal the book's theme and the author's agenda. Biblical books do not have these same components to help readers determine the author's goal, but they do have other ways to assist the reader in determining the book's themes. Instead of topic sentences and a table of contents, biblical authors carefully selected what content they wanted to include on the "Launching Pad" to introduce their overall thematic goals for the book.

So, as readers, we should slow down and ponder the book's early content and see what themes are introduced. The author is leaving "breadcrumbs" in the early content so that the reader is prepared for a fuller development of those themes later in the book.

BIBLICAL EXAMPLES OF "LAUNCHING PAD"

The first chapters of Genesis contain clear examples of this technique. Since Genesis is the fountainhead of Scripture, it is no wonder that its opening chapters contain many of the grand themes—not just of Genesis, but of the entire Bible (creation, the image of God, sin, etc.).

EXAMPLES OF HOW GENESIS 1–3 SETS UP THEMES DEVELOPED LATER IN THE PENTATEUCH	
Genesis 1–3	**Genesis 5–Deuteronomy 33**
Genesis 1:10, 28—importance of land (especially "dry land")	Genesis 8:14; Exodus 14:16, 22, 29; Joshua 3:17; 2 Kings 2:8
Genesis 1:11–12—stress on boundaries "according to their kind" and separation	Exodus 26:33; Leviticus 19:19; 20:24; Numbers 8:14
Genesis 1:26—importance of image	Genesis 5:3; 9:6
Genesis 1:22, 28; 2:3—importance of blessing	Genesis 9:1; 25:11; 35:9; 47:10; 48:20; Exodus 23:25; Deuteronomy 28; 33:1
Genesis 3—consequence of sin results in curse	Genesis 4:11; 9:25; Numbers 5:18–24; Deuteronomy 27
Genesis 3:21—change of clothes represents transitions	All throughout Joseph's life in Genesis; Exodus 28:4–43; Numbers 20:28

In Genesis 4, we read about the first account of life after the fall. The author of Genesis could have selected a variety of stories to share. For instance, we could have heard more of what happened between Adam and Eve after the fall—what they wore and ate, where they lived, etc. Instead, the text zeroes in on two siblings, Cain and Abel, who do not get along. We read about how they both brought an offering to the Lord, and the Lord says to Cain, "If you do well, will you not be accepted?" (v. 7). Cain worries about being a "wanderer" after he is punished for killing his brother Abel.

This highlights one of the main themes in Genesis 4: sibling rivalry. What better way is there to introduce a key theme found throughout Genesis than by chronicling an example of it in the first family? This theme of sibling rivalry, introduced in the Cain and Abel account, is the first of many such rivalries in the book of Genesis: Abraham and Lot, Isaac and Ishmael, Esau and Jacob, Rachel and Leah, Joseph and his brothers. The author of Genesis 4 is subtly communicating that one of the most significant consequences of the fall is that it fractures families and kindles conflict in the home. In addition, Cain's worries about being a "wanderer" on the earth due to his sin is a preview of what is going to be seen in the book of Numbers, which contains a record of Israel's wilderness wanderings.

So, the account of Cain and Abel not only contains historical information about life after the fall, but it also acts as a mini thematic table of contents for the rest of the five books of Moses (the Pentateuch). Such is the richness and beauty of God's Word!

HOW THE CAIN AND ABEL ACCOUNT IN GENESIS 4 THEMATICALLY SETS UP THE FIVE BOOKS OF THE PENTATEUCH		
	Genesis 4	**Books of the Pentateuch**
Gen. 4:9	"Then the LORD said to Cain, 'Where is Abel your brother?' He said, 'I do not know; am I my brother's keeper?'"	The concept of sibling rivalry/family strife as a result of sin is a major theme throughout the book of **Genesis**. This can be seen in friction between Abraham and Lot, Isaac and Ishmael, Jacob and Esau, Rachel and Leah, and Joseph and his brothers.
Gen. 4:3	"In the course of time Cain brought to the LORD an **offering** of the fruit of the ground."	The text of Genesis 4 gives no details about the instructions that were given to Cain and Abel regarding worship and sacrifices. The book of **Leviticus** will later fill in those details for the reader but they are primed to be ready for that discussion with that theme being dropped early here in Genesis.

Gen. 4:14	Cain says, "I shall be a fugitive and a **wanderer** on the earth, and whoever finds me will kill me."	The consequence of not obeying the Lord is exile and restless wandering which prefigures the forty years of wilderness wandering the Israelites experienced in the book of **Numbers** as a result of their sin.
Gen. 4:7	"If you do **well**, will you not be accepted?"	What it means to do "well" (Hebrew *tov*) in order to be accepted by the Lord is not defined here but will be further developed in the law codes of **Exodus** and **Deuteronomy**. "Be careful to obey all these words that I command you, that it may go *well* with you and with your children after you forever, when you do what is good and right in the sight of the LORD your God" (Deut. 12:28).

The lack of details shared by biblical authors can be puzzling. For instance, we are not told about the instructions that Cain and Abel were given regarding sacrifices. Were they told specific instructions about what kind of sacrifice they should bring (animal or crops)? Were they told to build an altar and how to prepare their offering?

What is the purpose behind this vagueness and lack of specificity? Perhaps the author (Moses) is laying the foundation and dropping a breadcrumb for readers to pique their curiosity regarding worship and sacrifices—a whole book is forthcoming (Leviticus) that will answer that question in more detail. As for the meaning of the Lord's statement that "if you do well, will you not be accepted?" (Gen. 4:7), there are two forthcoming books (Exodus and Deuteronomy) written by the same author that will specifically answer that question.

Isaiah is another book where this technique is evident. The first two chapters lay out the key themes for the entire book. Typically, a prophetic book would contain details of that prophet's call to service in the opening content (e.g., Ezekiel 1 and Jeremiah 1), but in the book of Isaiah, the call is not recorded until chapter 6. So, the book of Isaiah jumps right in with the prophet's message and delays the description of Isaiah's call (see chapter 10 for more on "Out of Order") to highlight the book's themes in Isaiah 1–5 over the credentials of the prophet. Therefore, the "Launching Pad" material in this book is intentionally placed up front. Here are some ways in which the early content of Isaiah serves as a table of contents for the entire book:

HOW ISAIAH 1–2 SETS UP THE REST OF THE BOOK OF ISAIAH		
	Isaiah 1–2	Isaiah 3–66
1:1	"The vision of Isaiah the son of Amoz, which he saw concerning Judah and Jerusalem in the days of Uzziah, Jotham, Ahaz, and Hezekiah, kings of Judah."	Sets up for Isaiah having significant interaction with kings of Judah, especially Ahaz (Isa. 7) and Hezekiah (Isa. 36–39)
1:2	"Hear, O heavens, and give ear, O earth; for the LORD has spoken: 'Children have I reared and brought up, but they have rebelled against me.'"	Echoes back to Genesis 1–3 with reference to heavens and earth and rebellion against God, but also introduces the theme of disobedience, a key theme in the book
1:3	"The ox knows its owner, and the donkey its master's crib, but Israel does not know, my people do not understand."	Surfaces another key theme of Isaiah—ignorance of the ways of God
1:4	"Ah, sinful nation, a people laden with iniquity, offspring of evildoers, children who deal corruptly! They have forsaken the LORD, they have despised the Holy One of Israel, they are utterly estranged."	Introduces the reader to one of Isaiah's favorite names for God: "the Holy One of Israel"—a phrase he uses over twenty-five times throughout the book; serves also to prepare the reader for the call scene of Isaiah 6, where God's holiness is prominent

1:5–6	"Why will you still be struck down? Why will you continue to rebel? The whole head is sick, and the whole heart faint. From the sole of the foot even to the head, there is no soundness in it, but bruises and sores and raw wounds; they are not pressed out or bound up or softened with oil."	Although not as clear, this could be preparing the reader for the "suffering servant" (especially Isa. 53) where that figure takes the punishment that is really fitting for rebellious Israel
1:7	"Your country lies desolate; your cities are burned with fire; in your very presence foreigners devour your land; it is desolate, as overthrown by foreigners."	Prepares the reader for all the foreign nation and judgment oracles within the book (Isa. 13–24)
1:8	"And the daughter of Zion is left like a booth in a vineyard, like a lodge in a cucumber field, like a besieged city."	Sets the table for Isaiah 5, which is the song of the vineyard
1:16–17	"Wash yourselves; make yourselves clean; remove the evil of your deeds from before my eyes; cease to do evil, learn to do good; seek justice, correct oppression; bring justice to the fatherless, plead the widow's cause."	Surfaces the typical spiritual/ethical injunctions found throughout the Prophets; this not only sets up Isaiah, but also is a great "Launching Pad" theme for all the major and minor prophets and why Isaiah is at the head of all the prophetical books even though he is not chronologically the first prophet
1:18	"Come now, let us reason together, says the LORD: though your sins are like scarlet, they shall be as white as snow; though they are red like crimson, they shall become like wool."	Anticipates passages like Isaiah 55, where another invitation is issued

| 2:2–5 | "It shall come to pass in the latter days that the mountain of the house of the LORD shall be established as the highest of the mountains, and shall be lifted up above the hills; and all the nations shall flow to it, and many peoples shall come, and say: 'Come, let us go up to the mountain of the LORD, to the house of the God of Jacob, that he may teach us his ways and that we may walk in his paths.' For out of Zion shall go forth the law, and the word of the LORD from Jerusalem. He shall judge between the nations, and shall decide disputes for many peoples; and they shall beat their swords into plowshares, and their spears into pruning hooks; nation shall not lift up sword against nation, neither shall they learn war anymore. O house of Jacob, come, let us walk in the light of the LORD." | Prepares the reader for themes found in the second half of Isaiah, where the Lord will fulfill His promises of blessings and peace for the nation of Israel at some point in the future |

The "Launching Pad" content of Isaiah is a wonderful preview of coming attractions within the whole book. Good authors have strong introductions with a clear thesis statement. These up-front teasers prepare the reader for further development of themes that are briefly mentioned at the start.

This also helps explain the placement of the book of Isaiah at the head of the prophetic books in the Old Testament (Isaiah to Malachi). It can also serve as a thematic introduction to all the Prophets, since it introduces most of the major themes found within that section of the canon.

As shown above, even if this technique is not present in every book of the Bible, this "Launching Pad" device is prevalent enough in the Scriptures that readers should pay close attention to what is communicated in the first chapters of a book and take time to ponder the thematic implications. After completing a book, readers should then review the beginning of it and reflect on how that initial content is revisited later.

The Declaration of Independence is a key founding document of the United States. The title alone sets a key theme for the rest of the document, but also notice how the following sentence in the second paragraph serves as a launching pad for the rest of the declaration and nation that it birthed: "We hold these truths to be self-evident, that all men are created equal, that they are endowed by their Creator with certain unalienable Rights, that among these are Life, Liberty and the pursuit of Happiness."

Individual books of the Bible often have a launching pad with a similar literary and rhetorical effect. Focusing on the up-front content gives us a taste of the textual feast the author has set before us and enhances our enjoyment of the rest of the book.

GO and IMPLEMENT

Take time to examine each of the following examples.

BOOK OF THE BIBLE	THEME INTRODUCED
Proverbs 1:1–7	These early verses describe the purpose of the book and the underlying theme of the book.
Ezekiel 1	Ezekiel's wheel vision sets up the book's major themes: 1) a book full of visions (2, 37, 40–48) 2) God's mobility (11) 3) Glory from beginning (1) to end (40–48, especially 43)[7]

59

Hosea 1–3	Hosea's introduction touches upon the major themes of the book and doubles as a great setup for all the minor prophets, since it is the first one canonically.
Psalms 1–2	Psalms 1 and 2 provide a perfect thematic introduction to the entire book and serve as a pragmatic goal for all readers: meditate on the Scriptures (Ps. 1) and worship the King (Ps. 2).[8]
Luke 1–2	Simeon's speech in Luke 2:29–34 touches upon key themes for the whole book when he declares: "'*For my eyes have seen your salvation* that you have prepared in the presence of *all peoples*, a light for revelation to the Gentiles, and for glory to your people Israel.' . . . And Simeon blessed them and said to Mary his mother, 'Behold, this child is appointed for the *fall and rising of many in Israel*, and for a sign that is opposed.'" Simeon's statement foregrounds salvation of both Jew and Gentile through Jesus and stresses the notion that the Messiah will be the catalyst for blessing and stumbling to His people.

FOR FURTHER STUDY

Amit, Yairah. *Reading Biblical Narratives: Literary Criticism and the Hebrew Bible.* Minneapolis: Fortress Press, 2001. (Chapter 4)

Hooker, Morna D. *Beginnings: Keys That Open the Gospels.* Eugene, OR: Wipf & Stock, 2010.

5

Beautiful Bookends

SUMMARY: Look for content at the beginning of a Bible book that is repeated at the end of the same book. This technique is a literary rhetorical device in which the author introduces an element at the beginning of a book and then returns to it at the end, thus bookending the intervening material.

PREVALENCE: This appears in all sorts of biblical books, so it is not limited by genre or Testament. It is also used within books to mark off chapters or sections.

INSTRUCTION: Read the first part of a Bible book and then read the last part (skipping over the middle), looking for repeated elements (words, phrases, people, objects, places, etc.). Once the bookends are detected, it will require a reading of the entire book to look for how the bookends are helpful thematically for content in the middle.

VALUE/PAYOFF: Functionally, it serves as a sort of parenthesis to artistically enclose material. Structurally, it brings closure and brackets off the content in the middle in an aesthetic way. Practically, it foregrounds themes and connections that the biblical author intentionally wants the reader to contemplate as they read the book.

CHALLENGES: Some of the bookends may not be lexical (which are easier to detect), but rather, conceptual. It may not always be easy to distinguish a true bookend from coincidental repetition. There will be varying degrees of certainty and subjectivity as to what the intent or value of the bookend may be for the reader.

EXAMPLES FROM NONBIBLICAL WORKS:

Forrest Gump **(1994 film):** The feather floating at the beginning and end of the film.

1917 **(2019 film):** The soldier resting against a tree at the beginning and end of the film.

Beauty and the Beast **(1991 film):** The stained-glass image at the beginning and ending of the animated film.

I have a number of bookends on my library shelves in my offices at school and home. Most of them are nothing fancy—shiny black metal frames that hardly draw attention to themselves because they are thin and blend in to the surroundings. I do have a few fancy marble bookends (okay, actually faux alabaster marble) of Assyrian lamassu figures that are highly decorative and draw attention even over the books in between them. Biblical authors can also frame the contents of their book by inserting matching literary enclosures at the beginning and ending of their work—beautiful literary bookends.

One way to increase your delight as you read the Bible is to look for how biblical authors bracket similar content at the beginning and end of their books. This chapter mainly focuses on the outer edges of biblical books, but bookends can also be seen at the beginning and end of smaller units—whether it be a verse, paragraph, or passage. This increases your satisfaction level once you see their presence, but they also set a thematic frame so you can observe a truth that the biblical author is stressing, which is an aid to interpreting the book in line with authorial intent.

The technical term for this literary device is *inclusio* (also known as "envelope structure"), which is a compositional style where content at the initial part of a passage is repeated again at the end. This feature helps establish literary boundaries and provides a sense of closure to a composition. In some ways it functions as a picture frame encircling the body of the work, helping to set thematic boundaries.

Remember that the original audience for the biblical books was most likely listening to the text with their ears rather than reading it with their eyes, so this technique would aid a listener's ability to distinguish units.

Once we find a bookend, then we can reflect on why that particular bookend was utilized. This might seem problematic because it requires us to try to determine why that bookend is selected even though the biblical author does not explicitly spell out why it is there and what purpose it serves. However, since the bookends are intentionally placed there by the biblical author, it is safe to assume that they serve not only as a structural bracketing device but also as a rhetorical signal to readers, highlighting a theological point or theme.

BIBLICAL EXAMPLES OF "BEAUTIFUL BOOKENDS"

In the opening chapter of Mark's gospel, when John the Baptist baptized Jesus, He saw "the heavens being torn open" (Mark 1:10). Then at the end of Mark's gospel during the crucifixion scene, "the curtain of the temple was torn in two, from top to bottom" (Mark 15:38). These two "torn" events bookend the public ministry of Jesus and give a divine sense of approval to the whole life and ministry of Christ. In addition, another bookend is used: a verbal declaration that Jesus is the Son of God (Mark 1:11; 15:39).[9]

Mark 1:10 And when he came up out of the water, immediately he saw the heavens being <u>torn open</u> and the Spirit descending on him like a dove.

Mark 15:38 And the curtain of the temple was <u>torn in two</u>, from top to bottom.

Mark 1:1 the beginning of the gospel of Jesus Christ, the <u>Son of God</u>.
Mark 1:11 And a voice came from heaven, "You are my beloved <u>Son</u>; with you I am well pleased."

Mark 15:39 And when the centurion, who stood facing him, saw that in this way he breathed his last, he said, "Truly this man was the <u>Son of God</u>!"

After recognizing the existence of these bookends, now the reader can reflect on how they function in the book of Mark. Mark intentionally selected both bookends because they aid in helping the reader identify key themes of the book. The heavens being torn open at Jesus' baptism, followed by a divine pronouncement that Jesus is the Son, is matched at the end of Jesus' ministry on earth by the tearing of the temple curtain, which is followed by a declaration that Jesus is "the Son of God" by a Gentile. The centurion's declaration should be the same response of all readers of Mark's gospel after reading the book.

Another New Testament example is the book of Romans. In the opening and closing paragraphs, Paul uses the phrase "obedience of faith" as bookends to his epistle (1:5 and 16:26). This helps readers to understand that Paul is not just stressing faith alone but also the outworking of that faith in faithful obedience. This is seen in how he crafts the content of the book by first focusing on faith and belief (Rom. 1–11) and then behavior (Rom. 12–16).

Also, Romans 1:2–3 stresses a messianic focus on David's lineage, and in Romans 15:12, Paul comes full circle and quotes the Old Testament prophet Isaiah, addressing that same concept.

OPENING BOOKEND	CLOSING BOOKEND
Romans 1:2–3 which he promised beforehand through his **prophets** in the holy Scriptures, concerning his Son, who was **descended from David** according to the flesh.	**Romans 15:12** And again **Isaiah** says, "The **root of Jesse** [father of David] will come, even he who arises to rule the Gentiles; in him will the Gentiles hope."
Romans 1:5 through whom we have received grace and apostleship to bring about the **obedience of faith** for the sake of his name among **all the nations**.	**Romans 16:26** but has now been disclosed and through the prophetic writings has been made known to **all nations**, according to the command of the eternal God, to bring about the **obedience of faith**.

This bookend device is found repeatedly throughout Scripture and in all genres (poetry, narrative, epistles). Below are just some of the examples of this literary structure and the thematic implications they invoke:

BOOK OF THE BIBLE	OPENING BOOKEND	CLOSING BOOKEND
Joshua	**1:7–8** Only **be strong** and very courageous, being careful to do according to all the law that **Moses my servant commanded you. Do not turn from it to the right hand or to the left,** that you may have good success wherever you go. This **Book of the Law** shall not depart from your mouth, but you shall meditate on it day and night, so that you may be careful to do according to all that is written in it. For then you will make your way prosperous, and then you will have good success. **1:12–18** And to the **Reubenites, the Gadites, and the half-tribe of Manasseh** Joshua said, "Remember the word that **Moses the servant of the LORD commanded you,** saying, 'The LORD your God is providing you a place of rest and will give you this land.' Your wives, your little ones, and your livestock shall remain in the land that **Moses gave you beyond the Jordan,** but all the men of valor among you shall pass over armed **before your brothers** and shall help them, until the LORD gives rest to your brothers as he has to you, and they also take possession of the land that the LORD your	**23:6** Therefore, **be very strong** to keep and to do all that is written in the **Book of the Law of Moses, turning aside from it neither to the right hand nor to the left.** **22:1–5** At that time Joshua summoned the **Reubenites and the Gadites and the half-tribe of Manasseh,** and said to them, "You have kept all that **Moses the servant of the LORD commanded you** and have obeyed my voice in all that I have commanded you. You have not forsaken your brothers these many days, down to this day, but have been careful to keep the charge of the LORD your God. And now the LORD your God has given rest to **your brothers,** as he promised them. Therefore turn and go to your tents in the land where your possession lies, which **Moses the servant of the LORD gave you on the other side of the Jordan.** Only be very careful to observe the commandment and the law that **Moses the servant of the LORD commanded you,** to love the LORD your God, and to walk in all his ways and to keep his commandments and to cling to him and to serve him with all your heart and with all your soul."

God is giving them. Then you shall return to the land of your possession and shall possess it, the land that Moses the servant of the LORD gave you beyond the Jordan toward the sunrise." And they answered Joshua, "All that you have commanded us we will do, and wherever you send us we will go. Just as we obeyed Moses in all things, so we will obey you. Only may the LORD your God be with you, as he was with Moses! Whoever rebels against your commandment and disobeys your words, whatever you command him, shall be put to death. Only be strong and courageous."

These bookends accentuate the point that Joshua's generation could be characterized as faithful and obedient because they followed the Book of the Law (Deuteronomy). This is illustrated by the actions of the tribes of Reuben, Gad, and the half-tribe of Manasseh. Modern readers should come away with the point that if they want to experience success (Josh. 1:8–9), they will likewise need to be faithful and obedient to God's commands.

Judges

1:1–2

After the death of Joshua, the people of Israel inquired of the LORD, **"Who shall go up first for us against the Canaanites, to fight against them?" The LORD said, "Judah shall go up;** behold, I have given the land into his hand."

20:18

The people of Israel arose and went up to Bethel and inquired of God, **"Who shall go up first for us to fight against the people of Benjamin?" And the LORD said, "Judah shall go up first."**

2:6

When Joshua dismissed the people, the people of Israel went **each to his inheritance** to take possession of the land.

21:24

And the people of Israel departed from there at that time, every man to his tribe and family, and they went out from there **every man to his inheritance.**

The first bookend here should be haunting to the reader. At the beginning of the book, the people of Israel are fighting the Canaanites, but at the end they are fighting against a fellow tribe! It also subtly reminds the reader that the tribe of Judah is the most faithful tribe, and it helps to set the stage for a major source of tension in the book of 1 Samuel in terms of leadership (Saul is from the tribe of Benjamin and David is from the tribe of Judah). The second bookend reveals that although there is a similarity to the beginning and ending of the book in that each tribe goes to their land inheritance, the reader is well aware that the period of Judges was not epitomized by "full" possession of the land (the task directed in Judg. 2:6) as the nation of Israel had to deal with both internal and external threats throughout the book and is now seen at the end of the book returning home and coexisting with the Canaanites.

Proverbs	1:7	31:30
	The **fear of the LORD** is the beginning of knowledge; fools despise wisdom and instruction.	Charm is deceitful, and beauty is vain, but a woman who **fears the LORD** is to be praised.

The bookends in Proverbs foreground the major theme of the book, which is the "fear of the LORD." "Wise" readers of this particular book should not only detect this theme but also put it into practice in day-to-day life, which is epitomized in the characteristics of the virtuous woman of Proverbs 31. This theme of the "fear of the LORD" is emphasized at the beginning and end of the book. This notion of "from beginning to end" is also captured by the use of the acrostic form (authors using successive letters of the alphabet in sequential order to signal completion) in the poem extolling the virtuous woman of wisdom in Proverbs 31.

Ezekiel	1:3	48:35
	the word of the LORD came to Ezekiel the priest, the son of Buzi, in the land of the Chaldeans by the Chebar canal, and the hand of the LORD was upon him **there**.	The circumference of the city shall be 18,000 cubits. And the name of the city from that time on shall be, The LORD Is **There**.

The bookends of Ezekiel present God as the one who is "there," which was meant not only to be a comforting theme to Ezekiel, who was an exile in Babylon, and a source of comfort to those contemplating the glory of the future temple, but also to modern-day readers who live in chaotic times.

John	1:1	20:28
	In the beginning was the Word, and the Word was with God, and the **Word was God**.	Thomas answered him, "My Lord and **my God**!"

1:7	20:31
He came as a witness, to bear witness about the light, **that all might believe through him.**	but these are written so that you may believe that Jesus is the Christ, the Son of God, **and that by believing you may have life in his name.**

These bookends stress the fact that Jesus was indeed God and that belief in Jesus is John's goal for those who are exposed to his words. Hopefully readers of this book will come to the same exuberant conclusion that Thomas comes to after reading John's magnificent work on the life and ministry of Jesus!

Colossians	1:9–10	4:5
	And so, from the day we heard, we have not ceased to pray for you, asking that you may be filled with the knowledge of his will in all spiritual wisdom and understanding, so as to **walk in a manner worthy of the Lord,** fully pleasing to him: bearing fruit in every good work and increasing in the knowledge of God.	**Walk in wisdom toward outsiders,** making the best use of the time.

The bookends here highlight one of the major themes of the book of Colossians—believers are instructed to walk in a wise manner before the Lord and before the world. This epistle unpacks what that walk should look like in the body of the book, but it is beautifully framed at the beginning and end of it.

1 Timothy	1:3	6:3
	As I urged you when I was going to Macedonia, remain at Ephesus so that you may charge certain persons not to **teach any different doctrine.**	If anyone **teaches a different doctrine** and does not agree with the sound words of our Lord Jesus Christ and the teaching that accords with godliness...

These bookends clearly identify a major theme that Paul is stressing in this book, which is that readers should adhere to sound doctrine and avoid those who don't. Modern readers, after reading this book, should recommit to knowing and living out the implications of sound doctrine if they truly want to apply this book.

This device is also used within sections of books, for example, in the Sermon on the Mount (Matt. 5:17; 7:12) and Jesus' public ministry (Luke 4:18–20; 19:10).

The daughters of Zelophehad bracket off the wilderness wandering period after the second census (Num. 27:1–11; 36:1–12), which highlights their faith in the promises of God as compared to the unbelieving generation before.

Bookends are also used in some individual chapters, such as Psalm 8 and Psalm 145.

Sometimes the bookend is more thematic than it is literal in words or phrases. For example, in the early chapters of Matthew, the wealthy magi bring gifts to Jesus (2:11), and near the end of the book, the wealthy Joseph of Arimathea gave his tomb for the body of Jesus after His death (27:57–60). Luke opens and closes by portraying events in the temple (1:5–23 with 24:50–53). Luke's gospel begins by mentioning a decree from Caesar Augustus (2:1), and he concludes his second book (the book of Acts) with Paul getting ready to testify to Caesar (28:19).

In a fascinating way, bookends are also found in the entirety of the canon of Scripture. Compare repeated elements in Genesis 1–3 with Revelation 20–22.

GENESIS–REVELATION BOOKENDS	
Genesis	Revelation
"God created the **heavens and the earth**" (1:1)	"Then I saw a **new heaven and a new earth**" (21:1)
"the darkness he called **Night**" (1:5)	"there will be no **night** there" (21:25); "And **night** will be no more" (22:5)
"and the waters that were gathered together he called **Seas**" (1:10)	"and the **sea** was no more" (21:1)

"And God made the **two great lights**" (1:16)	"And the city has no need of **sun or moon** to shine on it" (21:23)
"**A river** flowed out of Eden to water the garden" (2:10)	"Then the angel showed me the **river** of the water of life" (22:1)
"for in the day that you eat of it you shall surely **die**" (2:17)	"and **death** shall be no more" (21:4)
"Now the **serpent** was more crafty.... 'Did God actually say, "You shall not eat of any tree in the garden"?' (3:1)	"And he seized the dragon, that ancient **serpent**, who is the devil and Satan . . . and threw him into the pit, and shut it and sealed it over him, so that he might not deceive the nations any longer" (20:2–3)
"The LORD God said to the serpent, "Because you have done this, **cursed** are you above all livestock and above all beasts of the field; on your belly you shall go" (3:14)	"No longer will there be anything **accursed**" (22:3)
"To the woman he said, "I will surely multiply your **pain** in childbearing; in **pain** you shall bring forth children" (3:16)	"neither shall there be mourning, nor crying, nor **pain** anymore" (21:4)
"he placed the **cherubim** and a flaming sword that turned every way to guard the way to the **tree of life**" (3:24)	"Then came one of the seven **angels** who had the seven bowls full of the seven last plagues and spoke to me, saying, 'Come, I will show you the Bride, the wife of the Lamb'" (21:9) "so that they may have the right to the **tree of life**" (22:14)

Not only are these bookends beautiful in design, but they also serve to highlight the Edenic state that humanity was placed into at the creation of the world and will have the opportunity to return to at the culmination of human history. What is also amazing is that two different human authors under divine inspiration (Moses and the apostle John) were involved in making these bookends, which aesthetically close the loop on the entire canon.

My family and I enjoy participating in themed escape rooms.

A team of individuals is escorted through a door into a locked room and, in order to escape, must solve a series of puzzles within a time limit. An attendant shares vital information at the start of the experience that is critical for successful completion. Teams begin and end in the same place, and there is something satisfying when you walk out the same door that you entered, having completed the challenge victoriously.

Similarly, by identifying bookends we can enjoy the Bible more as we look for clues given at the beginning of books that are matched and framed with how the book ends. These parallels have embedded within them a key to help unlock what is in the middle so that one can come full circle. Identifying these bookends is a simple and effective technique for us to incorporate in our Bible reading. This technique can pay instant dividends and help us maintain focus and be more active readers of God's Word as we identify and apply the author's thematic thread.

GO and IMPLEMENT

JOSHUA: Look at Joshua 1:7–8 and 23:6 and reflect on how these verses not only bracket the book but identify one of the central themes of the book. Do the same for 1:12–18 and 22:1–5 to see mirrored content at the beginning and end.

MATTHEW: One of the clearest examples of bookends is in the gospel of Matthew. Investigate how 1:23 connects with 28:20 and provides one of Matthew's central tenets for the book. See how it is also reflected by outsiders who declare Jesus to be King (2:2; 27:37), foregrounding another key theme of the book.

FOR FURTHER STUDY

Deppe, Dean B. *The Theological Intentions of Mark's Literary Devices*. Eugene, OR: Wipf and Stock, 2015.

Hooker, Morna D. *Endings: Invitations to Discipleship*. Peabody, MA: Hendrickson, 2003.

6

Object Lessons

SUMMARY: Look for objects or props that are mentioned in the biblical text that serve a narrative function for readers by highlighting an individual's character traits or advancing the plot of the account.

PREVALENCE: This literary device is not all that common, but when it is used (and noticed), it provides readers with rewarding insights. It is predominantly a device used within narratives since it is often connected to plot and characterization.

INSTRUCTION: Identify objects within the text that are repeatedly associated with a biblical character, and then reflect on how the characteristics of that prop serve a literary narrative function beyond just their physical reality.

VALUE/PAYOFF: On a structural level, props help provide a cohesive element to the narrative and help bind components of an account into a larger metanarrative. Thematically, these props aid in developing a trait of the individual's character and provide a window into the overall plot that the biblical author is advancing.

CHALLENGES: This technique is more subtle and implicit. It requires readers to pay attention to detail to determine whether there is a potential correlation between the object and the characters within the narrative. It is not always easy to determine when a prop rises to serve a narrative or symbolic function.

EXAMPLES FROM NONBIBLICAL WORKS:

- Fedora and bull whip in Indiana Jones

- Light saber with Jedi knights in Star Wars

- Rings in *The Lord of the Rings*

- Mirrors in the Harry Potter series

- Yellow hat in Curious George books

- Dorothy's silver (ruby red in the film) slippers in *The Wizard of Oz*

In my neighborhood, houses commonly have flags on display in front of their homes. Some homes have American flags. Others have flags of various professional or college sports teams, prominently declaring their allegiance to their favorite team. Still others display flags supporting various causes or representing the academic institutions from which they graduated, showing pride in their alma maters. The flags are physical objects that communicate core values of the occupants of those homes. The logos or words emblazoned on them correspond closely and symbolically to the occupants of that house.

Biblical authors can also incorporate objects with characters to artfully and playfully symbolize that person's values or a key trait that they possess. By noticing these object lessons as we read the Bible, we can increase our delight as we see the care that the biblical authors used to craft the content of their books.

Any physical objects that function as a part of the backdrop in cinema, stage productions, or literary works are called "props" (short for "property"). On occasion, there are props that serve a narrative function beyond their mere physical existence and ability to add detail to a composition. Some props are so intertwined with a character that it is difficult to disassociate that prop from that character.

Keeping in mind that biblical authors were selective with the details they included, objects that are mentioned deserve careful attention by the reader to see if they add to the development of the plot and characterization. Props can be animate (goats or donkeys) or inanimate objects (fire, wells, rocks).

BIBLICAL EXAMPLES OF "OBJECT LESSONS"

Patriarchs in Genesis

Intriguingly, each of the patriarchs in Genesis has a prop that is associated with him. These props appear to be intentionally connected to each individual patriarch in Genesis because we rarely see these objects associated with the other patriarchs. For instance, we never read about the type of clothes that Abraham or Isaac wear, but we have multiple references to clothes in Joseph's life. Jacob's life is full of encounters with rocks and stones, but there are no scenes involving them in either Isaac's or Joseph's life.

PATRIARCH	OBJECT/PROP	TEXTS	SIGNIFICANCE
Abraham	Trees	Oaks of Moreh in Schechem (Gen. 12:6–7) Oaks of Mamre in Hebron (Gen. 13:14–18) Mt. Moriah (wood brought) in Jerusalem (Gen. 22) Abraham shows hospitality to two guests under a tree (Gen. 18:1, 4, 8) Abraham plants a tamarisk tree in Beersheba (Gen. 21:33) Abraham purchases a cave, field, and trees at Machpelah (Gen. 23:17)	Trees make for a fitting prop with Abraham. A number of connections are possible. Since Abraham is the start of a new lineage it makes sense that a tree is used (family tree with seeds). In addition, since Abraham is establishing a foothold in the land of Canaan, he is establishing roots throughout the land.
Isaac	Wells	Genesis 26:15, 18, 19, 22, 25, 32	There is only one chapter (Gen. 26) where Isaac appears on the stage away from the shadow of his father or his sons, and wells are frequently mentioned. Isaac is the child of promise and never leaves the land of Canaan. Everything he does in conjunction with the land is blessed by God, so much so that he has abundant crops (Gen. 26:12) and plenty of water (as seen in the repeated reference to numerous productive wells even in the arid Negeb region in this chapter). The land promise of the Abrahamic covenant is seeing partial fulfillment in Isaac's life.

Jacob	Stones/ rocks	Puts a stone under his head as a pillow at Bethel (Gen. 28:11)	Jacob is a man who sleeps on stones, moves stones, and sets up stones as monuments.[10] Stones/rocks make for a perfect prop for Jacob. He is always contending with hard unyielding things/obstacles, so much so that when he speaks to Pharaoh later in life, he says my days have been "long and hard" (Gen. 47:9).
		After his "ladder" vision he sets up his pillow rock as a commemorative marker (Gen. 28:18, 22)	
		He rolls away the stone from the well when he meets Rachel (Gen. 29:2–3, 8–10)	
		Twenty years later he sets up a testimonial heap of stones with Laban as a mutual nonaggression pact (Gen. 31:45–52)	
		He sets up another pillar of stone at Bethel after God speaks to him (35:14)	
Joseph	Clothes/ garments	Joseph receives garment from father (37:3), stripped of it by his brothers (37:23)	Clothes/garments are a pivotal element throughout the Joseph narrative and they serve as an obvious prop. They appear at key transition points in the account when his status changes positively or negatively. Just as people have different clothing for different settings, so readers can track plot movements whenever Joseph changes his garments.[11]
		Joseph receives garment from Potiphar (implied) (39:4), stripped of his cloak by Potiphar's wife (39:12)	
		Joseph receives garment from prison warden (implied) (39:22), changed out of it when he appears before Pharaoh (41:14)	
		Joseph receives garment from Pharaoh (41:42); role is now reversed—he gives changes of clothes to his brothers (45:22)	

Moses and Water

Water is a prop that is repeatedly associated with Moses and helps to unite the whole Moses narrative. It plays a key role in his birth account (Ex. 2) and also plays a pivotal role in his premature death (Num. 20). Water often communicates both life and death and is used as such by the biblical authors. Notice how often water appears at key junctions in Moses' life:

- He should have been thrown into the Nile (Ex. 1:22)

- He is saved in a reed basket on the Nile (Ex. 2:3)

- Pharaoh's daughter drew him up out of the Nile (origin of his name) (Ex. 2:10)

- He meets his wife by a well of water (Ex. 2:15–16)

- First plague deals with water (Nile turns to blood) (Ex. 7:17)

- It is where he meets with Pharaoh for two of the plagues (Ex. 7:15; 8:20)

- Moses parts the water (Ex. 14:21)

- Moses strikes a rock to bring forth water (Ex. 17:6)

- Moses strikes a rock twice in disobedience but water still comes out (Num. 20:8–11)

OTHER TEXTS THAT CONTAIN PROPS		
Text	**Prop**	**Meaning**
Book of Genesis	**Goats** Jacob wears goat skins to deceive Isaac and get blessing Jacob uses goats in the spotted/solid scheme against Laban Joseph's brothers use the blood of a goat to deceive Jacob into thinking Joseph is dead A goat is used as payment in the Judah/Tamar deception narrative	Often when a goat is mentioned in the book of Genesis, deception is a part of the account (Gen. 27:9–16; 30–31; 37:31; 38:17). The sneaky nature of goats makes them an appropriate prop to use in accounts where deceit is an element in the text.
Genesis 18:1, 2, 10; 19:6, 9, 10, 11	**Door**	The use of doors in Genesis 18 and 19 invites the reader to see a contrast. Abraham ultimately "sees" the divine at his doorway because of his faith, whereas the men of Sodom are "blinded" at Lot's door because of their wickedness. Doors serve as an entryway both physically and spiritually.
John 18:18; 21:9	**Charcoal fire**	Peter denies Christ while warming his hands over a charcoal fire, and Jesus lovingly restores Peter while cooking a breakfast over a similar charcoal fire. Charcoal fire is only used two times in the New Testament and only here in these passages. This prop invites us to make connections between Peter's denial and Peter's restoration.

Sometimes a prop is similarly used in different accounts, but it provides a springboard for readers to look for overlap between those texts. For instance, household idols (called teraphim) are mentioned in both Jacob's and David's life. Readers would not automatically connect those two texts, but because teraphim are infrequently mentioned in the Old Testament, this prop serves as a link that invites us to look for other similarities between the two passages. Lo and behold, a vast number of undeniable links become evident as the following chart displays.

TERAPHIM AS A LINK BETWEEN GENESIS 29–31 AND 1 SAMUEL 18–19		
Similarity	**Jacob/Rachel**	**David/Michal**
Triad of family members	Laban, Jacob, Rachel	Saul, David, Michal
Love for spouse	Jacob loved Rachel (29:20)	Michal loved David (18:20, 28)
Daughter possesses teraphim	Rachel (31:19)	Michal (19:13)
Deception regarding teraphim	Rachel sat on them, claiming impurity (31:34–35)	Michal used it to pretend David was sick in bed (19:13–16)
Surreal success of son-in-law	Jacob multiplies flocks exponentially (30:43)	David kills Goliath and obtains Philistine foreskins
Double the bride price	Jacob served fourteen years to secure Rachel when he initially agreed to work seven (29:18, 27)	Saul offered Michal to David for a hundred Philistine foreskins, and he delivers two hundred (18:25–27)
Jealous treachery	Laban removed the striped and spotted male goats from Jacob's herds (30:35)	Saul hurled spear at David (19:19)
Flight and chase	Jacob flees Paddan-aram, and Laban pursues (31:17)	David flees from Saul and Saul pursued him (19:18, 20–22)
Manipulation by father of two sisters in marriage pacts	Jacob contracted for Rachel, but Laban gave him Leah (29:20–28)	Saul offers Merab to David but then she is given to Adriel, then offers Michal (18:17–21)

The teraphim prop serves as a linking object between two different accounts that, on the surface, seem unrelated. This invites readers to draw comparisons and contrasts. In these two texts, we see fathers-in-law who attempt to make their sons-in-law out to be the villains, but it is resourceful daughters who protect their husbands from treachery. The biblical authors use teraphim, which were sometimes used as idolatrous prognostication devices by pagans, as a clever instrument to ironically unmask and expose the real manipulators in these accounts—their fathers!

Biblical authors are selective with the details they share, so we should slow down while reading and pay attention to the objects that are mentioned, reflecting on how they might connect to a theme or character trait in the text, or how they might provide a link between different passages. Tracking "Object Lessons" is a fun way we can freshen up our Bible reading and enjoy God's Word as we observe how props can enhance our understanding of biblical characters and plotlines.

GO and IMPLEMENT

- Contemplate all the uses of Moses' staff/rod (and sometimes just his outstretched arm) for reasons why that object might be repeatedly mentioned in his life as compared to other individuals.

- We saw how clothing was a prop in Joseph's life for marking transitions. Look at how the same notion is conveyed in the parable of the prodigal son (Luke 15) and the demoniac in Luke 8.

FOR FURTHER STUDY

Alter, R. *The Art of Biblical Narrative*. 2nd ed. New York: Basic Books, 2011. (p. 66)

Berlin, A. *Poetics and Interpretation of Biblical Narrative*. Sheffield, UK: The Almond Press, 1983. (p. 34)

Fokkelman, J. P. *Narrative Art in Genesis: Specimens of Stylistic and Structural Analysis (2nd Ed.)*. Eugene, OR: Wipf & Stock, 2004.

Matthews, Victor H. "The Anthropology of Clothing in the Joseph Narrative." *Journal for the Study of the Old Testament* 20, no. 65 (1995): 25–36.

Resseguie, James L. *Narrative Criticism of the New Testament: An Introduction*. Grand Rapids: Baker, 2005. (pp. 105–108)

Ryken, Leland. *Words of Delight: A Literary Introduction to the Bible*. Grand Rapids: Baker, 1993. (pp. 101–102)

Small, Brian. *The Characterization of Jesus in the Book of Hebrews*. Leiden, The Netherlands: Brill, 2014. (p. 65)

7

Poetic Diamonds

SUMMARY: Look for when biblical authors switch from narrative mode to lyrical mode within the body of the text. This often foregrounds a theme present in the surrounding narrative text.

PREVALENCE: Although there are whole books of the Bible in poetic form (e.g., Psalms), this phenomenon only occurs within narrative books, mainly in the Old Testament. It also occurs in the gospel of Luke and the book of Revelation, and some long speeches (such as the Sermon on the Mount) are in lyrical form.

INSTRUCTION: Look for embedded poetic insets with narrative text and ponder how the main point of the lyrical material accentuates a theme that is present in the surrounding narrative text. In printed Bibles, this can be done rather easily if they use either indented lines or italics to distinguish poetry from narrative text type.

VALUE/PAYOFF: These poetic diamonds add "punch" to what is stated in the surrounding narrative text and allow readers a high degree of certainty that they are grasping a thematic or theological point that the biblical author desires to stress. This aids in determining a passage's big idea.

CHALLENGES: For the most part this one is easy to detect due to how printed Bibles display lyrical lines (e.g., indented text and/or italics). There is some degree of subjectivity in trying to determine the relationship of the poetic inset within the surrounding narrative in which it is contained. There are also some poetic diamonds that are not readily discernible as to how they thematically connect to the surrounding narrative (e.g., Num. 10:35–36; 21:17–18; 21:27–30), but perhaps deeper reflection will reveal the relationship.

EXAMPLES FROM NONBIBLICAL WORKS:

The Lord of the Rings by J. R. R. Tolkien: There are over sixty poems embedded throughout the Middle-earth literature, and they are integral to the story in that they capture the mood of the scene ("Lament of the Rohirrim"), characterize the one singing (Pippin's "Bath Song"), or foreground major themes ("The Road Goes Ever On").

Through the Looking-Glass by Lewis Carroll: The poem "Jabberwocky" epitomizes the theme of the book that literature or poetry does not have to be serious, and that nonsense can be just as entertaining.

Love's Labour's Lost by William Shakespeare: Poetic insets seem to play a major role in this play, especially the Spring and Winter poems that surface one of the work's major themes—from folly to wisdom.

Musicals, whether they be performed on film or on stage, are a form of theater combining music, songs, dancing, and dialogue. The emotional content is communicated through the words, music, and technical aspects as an integrated whole. When something is set to music or poetry, the result typically heightens the message of the surrounding content. The same phenomenon occurs in Scripture when embedded poetic insets ("Poetic Diamonds") are placed within narrative accounts to accentuate the text's thematic context.

Growing up, I had a paper route that required I get up early seven days a week to deliver the local newspaper to residents in my neighborhood. Every once in a while, I would bribe a friend of mine to deliver the paper on Saturdays so I could sleep in. My mother was not always aware of this arrangement, and one Saturday morning she came into my bedroom while I was taking advantage of a little bit of extra sleep and said, "Jim, it is time to wake up." She would then proceed to sing the line from the musical *Oklahoma!*: "Oh, what a beautiful mornin', oh, what a beautiful day."[12] My mother was heightening the implied message of "it's time to get up and get to work" by pairing it with a song to accentuate the message.

BIBLICAL EXAMPLES OF "POETIC DIAMONDS"

Many readers are aware of whole books of the Bible (such as Psalms) that are comprised entirely of lyrical content. We should also be alert to the presence of these poetic diamonds in the narrative books of Scripture. Instead of a transcript, view narrative texts more along the lines of a musical. It is more than just a narrative storyline. It is infused with other styles of literature such as poetry or lyrical language. Understanding these nuances pays dividends for readers by allowing us to experience the text not only in a cognitive way but also with the emotional heartbeat that the biblical authors sought to weave into their inspired work.

Genesis

Poetic diamonds can be found on the micro level (in chapters) and also on the macro level (in books). This technique is evident in the first book of the Bible. Notice these poetic diamonds in Genesis 1–9.

TEXT	NARRATIVE	POETIC DIAMOND
Genesis 1	1–26	27
Genesis 2	1–22	23
Genesis 3	1–13	14–19
Genesis 4	1–22	23–24
Genesis 5	1–28	29
Genesis 6–9	6:1–9:24	9:25–27

Here are the first four chapters visually presented with the poetic diamonds embedded in the surrounding narrative texts.

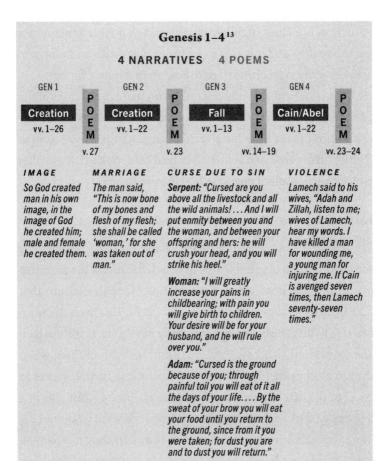

Genesis 1–4 [13]

4 NARRATIVES   4 POEMS

GEN 1		GEN 2		GEN 3		GEN 4	
Creation	P O E M	Creation	P O E M	Fall	P O E M	Cain/Abel	P O E M
vv. 1–26		vv. 1–22		vv. 1–13		vv. 1–22	
	v. 27		v. 23		vv. 14–19		vv. 23–24

IMAGE	MARRIAGE	CURSE DUE TO SIN	VIOLENCE
So God created man in his own image, in the image of God he created him; male and female he created them.	The man said, "This is now bone of my bones and flesh of my flesh; she shall be called 'woman,' for she was taken out of man."	Serpent: "Cursed are you above all the livestock and all the wild animals! . . . And I will put enmity between you and the woman, and between your offspring and hers: he will crush your head, and you will strike his heel." Woman: "I will greatly increase your pains in childbearing; with pain you will give birth to children. Your desire will be for your husband, and he will rule over you." Adam: "Cursed is the ground because of you; through painful toil you will eat of it all the days of your life. . . . By the sweat of your brow you will eat your food until you return to the ground, since from it you were taken; for dust you are and to dust you will return."	Lamech said to his wives, "Adah and Zillah, listen to me; wives of Lamech, hear my words. I have killed a man for wounding me, a young man for injuring me. If Cain is avenged seven times, then Lamech seventy-seven times."

Notice how the poetic diamond of Genesis 1 foregrounds one of the main themes of that chapter by emphasizing that humanity is made in the "image of God" (1:27). Genesis 2 contains a love ballad about marriage, which for humanity is the capstone of human relationship ordained by God (2:23). After the fall, the curse is constructed in lyrical style, foregrounding the consequences of disobedience to God (3:14–19). Lamech's lyrical excursion is a taunt highlighting the fact that violence is now a painful reality, and it is also a reminder that death and mayhem are now sadly even glamorized in heightened lyrical form.

These poetic diamonds not only punctuate the themes of the narratives in which they are embedded but also show the downward spiral from how lofty lyrical language extolling human dignity and marriage has now devolved into music that glorifies violence as a result of man's fall and disobedience.

Hannah's Song/Prayer in 1 Samuel 2:1–11

This passage functions as a poetic diamond that contains key thematic and theological truths to which the rest of the narrative portions of the book attest. For instance, Hannah exclaims that "the LORD ... brings low and he exalts" (2:7). This perfectly summarizes within the books of Samuel the raising up of faithful Saul and David and also how the Lord humbles both of them when they exhibit pride (2:3). This poetic diamond further serves as an example of a "Launching Pad" (see chapter 4), but also as a bookend (see chapter 5) to David's song found in 2 Samuel 22. The many verbatim parallels between Hannah's song in 1 Samuel 2:1–11 and David's song in 2 Samuel 22 (e.g., references to horns, rocks, thunder, and the anointed) are clearly intentional and show the function of poetic diamonds that illuminate themes of the surrounding narrative and add an emotional punch to what the author is stressing.

Simeon's Song in Luke 2:29–34

This song serves as a poetic diamond for Luke's gospel.

> "Lord, now you are letting your servant depart in peace,
>   according to your word;
> **for my eyes have seen your salvation**
>   that you have prepared in the presence of **all peoples**,
> a light for revelation to the Gentiles,
>   and for glory to your people Israel."
>
> ... And Simeon blessed them and said to Mary his mother,
> "Behold, this child is appointed for the **fall and rising of
> many in Israel**, and for a sign that is opposed."

The bold words in this passage punctuate Luke's key themes from his gospel just as Simeon's lyrical prayer foregrounds the salvation of both Jew and Gentile through Jesus and zeroes in on the notion that the Messiah will be the catalyst for blessing and stumbling to His people.

Identifying poetic diamonds is a way we can enjoy the Bible as we use our "ears" to listen to the interplay between narrative and embedded poetry and lyrical content. Just like my mother heightened the message she had for me by coupling it with a song, we can experience the same phenomenon in the pages of Scripture. Not only does this reveal the artistic beauty of God's Word, but it can be used to great personal benefit when you see how text and song identify key themes that the author desires to highlight for the reader. So turn up the volume on the musical interludes and let those lyrical pieces amplify the text's core message!

GO and IMPLEMENT

LUKE 1: This chapter contains another poetic diamond. See if you can discover how it summarizes the surrounding narrative portions of Luke and clues readers in on significant theological themes in the book.

1 CHRONICLES 4:9–10: Look for how this poetic diamond sets up a theme of how the different tribes went about land acquisition in 1 Chronicles 4–5.

NUMBERS 6:24–26: Investigate how the Aaronic blessing poetic diamond enhances the narrative context in which it is embedded.

DANIEL: Reflect on how the four poetic diamond prayers scattered throughout Daniel 2–6 (2:20–23; 4:3, 34–35; 6:26–27) emphasize certain divine attributes that are central themes for the book of Daniel.

FOR FURTHER STUDY

Fokkelman, Jan P. *Reading Biblical Narrative: An Introductory Guide.* Leiden, The Netherlands: Deo Publishing, 1999. (pp. 175–87)

Linafelt, Tod. *The Hebrew Bible as Literature: A Very Short Introduction.* Oxford: Oxford University Press, 2016. (Chapter 4)

Watts, James W. *Psalm and Story: Inset Hymns in Hebrew Narrative.* Sheffield, UK: Sheffield Academic Press, 1992.

8

Location, Location, Location

SUMMARY: Look for how the geographical locations mentioned in the text enhance the account. Treat the setting as you would a character—as a contributing participant with a voice. Oftentimes the setting evokes a certain mood and functions as a literary stage that gives readers a greater sense of certainty that they are reading the passage as the authors intended.

PREVALENCE: This device is very common. This is more evident in narrative books of the Bible since accounts depicted occur in a physical setting, but there are also examples of it in the poetic and prophetic portions of God's Word.

INSTRUCTION: Pay close attention to the information that the biblical author gives about the setting, and reflect on how and why that location plays a role in the account. Review previous events that took place in the same location, and think about whether or not there are similar elements to those accounts and any possible literary or thematic connections. Remember that settings often have symbolic connotations that the author is activating (which does not diminish the historical or physical context).

VALUE/PAYOFF: It is important for readers to notice the location of biblical events because setting is closely intertwined with the action and characters in revealing the author's plot development. It also helps the reader to emotionally enter into the overall mood of the account and connect more intimately with the characters because we often find ourselves in similar settings. Lastly, readers can deepen their engagement with the text by dovetailing the literal historical setting with the symbolic significance of the physical space.

CHALLENGES: Sometimes a geographical location is mentioned to anchor the account historically without necessarily invoking literary and theological connotations. Therefore, readers have to be careful not to over-spiritualize or read too much into the setting. Don't force symbolic significance without significant evidence that the author intends such a connection.

EXAMPLES FROM NONBIBLICAL WORKS:
The Rime of the Ancient Mariner by Samuel Taylor Coleridge: This poem utilizes two diverse settings (a joyful wedding scene and a ship traveling to the icy Antarctic) to great effect. The extreme contrast of the settings helps the readers experience the angst the mariner is going through.

The Lord of the Rings and *The Hobbit* by J. R. R. Tolkien: Tolkien is a master of using setting to create mood. For example, the locations of the Misty Mountains and Mirkwood Forest serve to heighten the tension and danger the characters experience. Continuous shifts in locations go hand in hand with the trials and triumphs the band encounters on their quests. The Shire is green and lush with gentle hills (peaceful) while Mordor is riddled with jagged mountains and sulfur pits (hostile).

Recently I had the privilege of traveling to Paris with my wife. We visited the Louvre Museum and the Eiffel Tower. The Louvre is a world-class display of art that stimulates the mind, whereas the Eiffel Tower tends to exude romance and issues of the heart. Needless to say, it was a satisfying trip mentally and emotionally. My wife and I had our picture taken in front of the fabled tower as a memento of our love for each other, celebrating our devotion through the years.

Some locations carry meaning beyond their geographical setting and conjure up certain moods and events that speak to the highs and lows of our human existence. Places like Gettysburg, Auschwitz, and Pearl Harbor invite deep introspection whenever they are visited or referenced, while other locations like the Grand Canyon, Plymouth Rock, and the Eiffel Tower evoke notions of greatness, hope, or romance.

Think about the geographical places that have shaped and

influenced who you are today: your hometown, the neighborhood you grew up in, the places you went to get away, the trips you took to distant places. I have spent most of my life in the Midwest in middle-class suburban neighborhoods and that has left a deep imprint on me. Living each year through the rhythm of four distinct (and sometimes harsh!) seasons has become ingrained in me that so that I can roll with the various and difficult "seasons" of life as I age.

Understanding the role that geography has in our lives can increase our delight in reading God's Word as we pay attention to the physical surroundings and locations of events in Scripture.

THE IMPORTANCE OF SETTING IN SCRIPTURE

The often-stated key to selling real estate is location, location, location. Where something happens is an important element to ponder as one reads any text, including Scripture. Many Bible readers tend to overlook the significance of setting in Scripture because they focus more on the characters and action. However, the setting itself can be seen as another character in the story. Settings can create a certain mood and help the reader visualize the scene.

When Jacob flees from his brother Esau after he took Esau's blessing, he comes close to the border of Israel and the text states that "he came to a certain place and stayed there that night, because the sun had set" (Gen. 28:11). It was there that he laid down upon a stone to sleep and had his dream about angels ascending and descending. He calls the name of the place Bethel. The next day he leaves the land and went "to the land of the people of the east" (29:1), where he spends the next twenty years.

Then, in Genesis 32, Jacob is returning home when, just before he crosses back into the land at the Jabbok River, he has a mysterious wrestling match, and his name is changed to Israel. He calls the name of the place "Penuel," and the text says that "the sun rose upon him as he passed Penuel" (Gen. 32:31).

So when Jacob left the land in fear in Genesis 28, the text explicitly states that "the sun had set," at that particular location (Bethel). Twenty years later he has another divine encounter at another place he named (Penuel) before reentering the land of Canaan. After the encounter, the text specifically states that the "sun rose." Clearly the sun set and rose each day for the twenty years he was away, but Moses only mentions the sunset and sunrise at the beginning and ending of Jacob's prodigal years away from the land. So, the subtle mood that the scene creates is that, for the time Jacob was away from the land, it was "nighttime," but when Jacob admits who he is and has a divine encounter (along with a name change), literally and symbolically there was a new day dawning in his life.

Some places have eerie and ominous overtones (e.g., cemeteries and old, decrepit houses) in modern storytelling. The same can be true of places mentioned in the Bible. Certainly, the mention of wilderness or storms at sea in the text creates some of those same bleak and foreboding "moods," not only for the characters but also for the readers of the passage.

Genesis 37 contains another example of how the mention of a place can create a certain sense of foreboding. When readers come to Genesis 37, there is a specific reference to a place

(Shechem) that acts as a red herring to the overall account. Joseph is sent out by Jacob to find out what is going on with his brothers since they have not come back home in a timely fashion. Young Joseph left Hebron and arrived at Shechem (Gen. 37:13–14). The mention of Shechem is a dead end since the brothers are not there, but there is a nameless individual who tells Joseph that he overheard them say they were going to Dothan. Joseph then leaves for Dothan and finds his brothers there, and the trajectory of Joseph's life takes a radical turn as he is sold as a slave to Midianites going down to Egypt.

The red herring reference of Shechem is intriguing because its mention is not that significant to the main storyline. Moses could have left it out and just simply recorded that Joseph set out and found his brothers shepherding their flocks at Dothan, omitting the mention of Shechem from the text. So what is the purpose of Moses' mention of Shechem in Genesis 37 if it really is not necessary in the grand scheme of things?

Here is where the previous mention of the geographical place comes into play. Prior to Genesis 37, we read of an earlier event that took place in Shechem in Genesis 34. It was at Shechem where Dinah, Jacob's daughter, was kidnapped and sexually violated. Dinah's brothers Simeon and Levi brutally murdered the men of Shechem as a vindictive act of revenge against the town. So the reference to what happened in Genesis 34 at Shechem should still be lingering in the mind of the reader when they come to read Genesis 37. An ominous mood looms at the mention of Joseph anywhere near that place, since the last time an offspring of Jacob was by themselves at Shechem, bad things happened. Moses is foreshadowing danger to the reader in Genesis 37 by mentioning that place, even if it is a red herring to the main action.

Even though the mention of Shechem seems like a geographical dead end, it is intentionally included to get the reader mentally prepared to expect another perilous action that will soon take place at Dothan. Joseph, who is by himself just as Dinah was when she ventured out on her own (and in the same vicinity), is about to step into a danger zone geographically.

OTHER SETTINGS THAT INFUSE MEANING INTO THE TEXT

Gardens

There is frequent mention of a garden/gardener (five times) in John 18–20. John is the only gospel writer who uses this term during Passion Week. It is intriguing that John seems to organize his gospel around themes from Genesis (e.g., Gen. 1:1 is echoed in John 1:1). Therefore, it seems thematically fitting that a garden, where intimate communion with God was available (Gen. 3:8) and where the first temptation took place, is now echoed geographically with the end of the public ministry of Jesus where He communed with the Father (John 17) and then enters a garden (John 18:1). It is there that He, in agony, requests the Father to let this cup pass from Him but is submissive to the Father's will to proceed to the cross. The setting of a garden is the backdrop for those two major events.

Wells

Wells are a geographical type scene in the Bible. A type scene involves a repetition of speech patterns and behaviors in analogous accounts. Repeatedly throughout the Scriptures, betrothals happen near wells (Gen. 24; 29; Ex. 2). In this particular type scene, a general pattern emerges. There is a prospective bridegroom (or an agent thereof) who travels to a distant land and meets his future spouse who is drawing water out of a local well. The future bride-to-be hurries home to share the news of the future husband's arrival, and a marriage arrangement ensues.

Mountains

In Matthew's gospel, mountains serve as a key geographical setting in the book. Just like Moses on Mount Sinai, the new Moses, Jesus, gives significant teaching from mountains (Matt. 5:1–11; 17:1–9; 24:1–3; 28:16–18).

So, when reading the Bible, keep your radar and GPS system activated to track the setting and geographical movement within the text. Look for ways that the location of the account not only enhances the plot but also subtly communicates significant overtones in addition to the physical and historical realities of what happened in that space. This is yet another way we can enjoy Scripture as a divinely authored literary masterpiece.

GO and IMPLEMENT

BORDER CROSSINGS: Look at the following chapters that involve border crossings and see how each is commemorated with a mark in the flesh: Genesis 32:22–32; Exodus 4:24–26; Joshua 3:1–5:3.

JERUSALEM: As you are reading Luke and Acts, look for ways that Luke moves toward Jerusalem with the death and resurrection of Jesus in Luke and then starts the book of Acts in Jerusalem, chronicling the geographical spread of the gospel to the ends of the earth.

FOR FURTHER STUDY

Brown, Jeannine K. *The Gospels as Stories: A Narrative Approach to Matthew, Mark, Luke, and John.* Grand Rapids: Baker, 2020. (pp. 80–81)

Rhoads, David, Joanna Dewey, and Donald Michie. *Mark as Story: An Introduction to the Narrative of a Gospel.* 3rd ed. Minneapolis: Fortress Press, 2012. (Chapter 3)

Ryken, Leland. *How Bible Stories Work: A Guided Study of Biblical Narrative.* Wooster, OH: Weaver Book Company, 2015. (Chapter 2)

Ryken, Leland. *Words of Delight: A Literary Introduction to the Bible.* Grand Rapids: Baker, 1993. (pp. 54–62)

9

Clock Management

SUMMARY: Track how the biblical author uses both time and pacing as a way to track what they are emphasizing in the text.

PREVALENCE: It is very commonplace. Since this is mainly a narrative phenomenon, it is commonly observed in historically focused books, although the principle is still the same in other genres of the Bible.

INSTRUCTION: Biblical authors sometimes insert enough timestamps embedded within the overall account to allow readers to have a fairly detailed timeline of events. In addition, while you are reading, slow down and take notice of the pacing of the events described in the account, looking for when the author speeds up the sequence or slows down the account to focus on a shorter period of time. You can often track accelerated pacing by observing the frequency and clustering of action verbs in close proximity to each other. A key element to track is the insertion of direct speech, which slows down the action to allow readers to ponder the importance of what was spoken.

VALUE/PAYOFF: Textual real estate is valuable. Biblical authors were selective about what to include in the text. As readers, we can see areas of emphasis and focal points when we pay attention to the difference between narration time and real time.

CHALLENGES: There are no major challenges other than the subjectivity involved in trying to determine the degree of emphasis on why an author slows down the tempo or accelerates it. Subjectivity is always going to be an issue for readers since biblical authors never explicitly state their rationale for the pacing of the account, but usually there are enough temporal markers embedded in the text to act as guardrails from drifting too far away from the author's intentions.

EXAMPLES FROM NONBIBLICAL WORKS:
"The Most Dangerous Game" by Richard Connell: This short story is fast-paced throughout as it intends to keep the tension and uncertainty at a high level. As a result, the modern reader literarily experiences the suspense of the human cat-and-mouse hunt.

Pride and Prejudice **by Jane Austen:** Austen inserts description and dialogue to slow down the pacing of the book, such as when Elizabeth's mother opines about her daughter's paramours or her description of the physical features of her suitors.

In many sports, a coach must be able to manage the clock if he wants to be successful. A football coach knows which plays will keep his offensive team out on the field longer to prevent giving the opposing team an opportunity to score, especially at the end of a game. A basketball coach knows when to call a timeout to slow the momentum and allow the players to compose themselves for the next stretch. A coach also knows the importance of watching the tape of an individual's performance after a game to improve their in-game skills for future competition. They also know the value of watching footage of their opponents' previous games to devise a game plan for that particular opponent. They will often fast-forward through much of the game and then use slo-mo to concentrate on critical moments in the game for further reflection and analysis.

In much the same way, biblical authors are also clock managers in that they can speed up or slow down the account to highlight a particular episode in a character's life. An astute reader will keep track of how the author is managing the clock of the narrative to see when periods pass by quickly (perhaps in just a few verses) and when the passage focuses on a short period of time. In either case, it is worthwhile for a reader to acknowledge the pace at which an author covers the action in the text and consider why certain periods of time are not given much attention or, conversely, why the author gives a lot of details for events that only take a short amount of time.

The best example of "Clock Management" is the gospel writers' handling of the life of Jesus. Luke 3:23 tells us that Jesus was about thirty when He began to do public ministry, and most scholars are in agreement that Jesus lived another three years after His baptism by John the Baptist until His crucifixion. Only Matthew and Luke contain information about Jesus' nativity, and there is little information about His childhood and early adult life except for the one incident when Jesus was twelve at the temple courts in Jerusalem (Luke 2:41–52). The bulk of the gospel record is on the three years of Jesus' public ministry, and a large percentage of that focus is on the passion narrative (the last eight days of Jesus' life).

GOSPEL	CHAPTERS DEVOTED TO PASSION WEEK	AMOUNT OF GOSPEL DEVOTED TO PASSION WEEK
Matthew	21–28	28%
Mark	11–16	37%
Luke	19–24	25%
John	12–20	38%

At least a quarter of each gospel is spent on details surrounding the last week or so of Jesus' life, and John even devotes seven chapters (John 13–19) to one day during that week! The gospel writers are not attempting to provide a full and complete biography of the entire life of Christ but are intentionally focusing on events that fit their thematic and theological purposes.

By looking at how the gospel writers "manage the clock," readers can more readily discern some of those purposes by considering when they speed up and especially when they slow down to focus on an event. The gospel writers' focus on the Passion Week helps us as readers see that a major theme of the Gospels is that Christ came to suffer and die on the cross for our sins, and His resurrection demonstrates our sins can be forgiven.

Another clear example of "Clock Management" is the account of Abraham in Genesis 12–24. According to the text, Abraham lives for 175 years (Gen. 25:7), yet in terms of literary real estate, the bulk of Genesis 12–25 focuses on only about twenty-five years of his life (ages 75–100). Even then, there is a thirteen-year gap (from the birth of Ishmael until he is circumcised) within that twenty-five year period. So the author (Moses) is not sharing a full biographical history of the entirety of Abraham's life but is mainly concerned with a twenty-five year period (and to an even smaller extent, only about twelve of those years due to the thirteen-year gap).

Moses really slows down the timeline in Genesis 22–23. Genesis 22 is the familiar account of Abraham nearly sacrificing his son Isaac, which consumes about a week's worth of actual time, and Genesis 23 is a fairly long and detailed account describing the purchase of the cave of Machpelah from the Hittites, which also takes place in a short period of time (within a few days at most).

This chart shows the difference between narration time and actual time in the life of Abraham.

Narration Time vs. Actual Time: Abraham

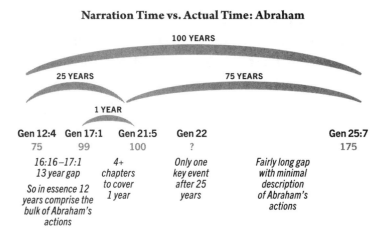

Even though Abraham lived 175 years, the book of Genesis covers only 100 of those years and then only focuses on his actions during a twelve-year stretch of his time on earth! Genesis 12–21 covers a twenty-five-year period, and there is a thirteen-year gap between Genesis 16:16 and 17:1. Readers then should be aware that they are not receiving a complete biography of Abraham's life, but only selected incidents from a relatively short period of time. Even though a major chunk of Abraham's life is not known to us, the author has managed the clock of this patriarch's life to include incidents that accomplish his thematic goal for the book. The author of Genesis wants us to focus on the progress (or lack thereof) of Abraham's faith in the promises of God.

Sometimes an author will specify a certain time of day when an event happened. An event can take place "early in the morning" (Gen. 22:3), at noon or the sixth hour (Acts 10:9; 22:6; John 4:6), at night (John 3:2), or the middle of the night (Ruth 3:8). At times, the author is seeking to communicate something by detailing what time of the day an event happened. Describing an event as happening "early in the morning" may connote that the character was demonstrating obedience. An event at noon is perhaps signaling that an event is done in the wide open so there can be no denial of its occurrence. Something taking place at night implies secrecy and perhaps even something sinister. Pay attention to time markers in the text and ponder why that level of detail may have been included by the author beyond just creating a factual timestamp.

I recently received a smartwatch as a Christmas gift. This technology is wonderful to monitor such things as the number of steps I take in a day or notify me when I receive a voice or text message. It can also provide a chart and visual display of my heart rate throughout the day or during certain activities. Another thing it does is remind me that I have been sedentary for too long, prompting me to get up and move around. I can get so focused on my work in front of a computer that I forget that my body needs to vary its routine.

This device helps me manage my time efficiently and track my heart rate throughout the day so that I can stay healthy. Similarly, by using this "Clock Management" technique, we can read and enjoy the Bible more as we pay close attention to how the author manages the literary clock and the pulse rate of the events. Catch some of the adrenaline rush that the characters experience or notice when time seems to stand still. Readers who focus on when the author speeds things up and slows things down are better able to track the moments in the account that the author is highlighting. It is those moments that are being stressed for greater reflection and can lead us to savor not just what the author is saying but how they are communicating it.

GO and IMPLEMENT

GENESIS 38: This chapter shows both the speeding up of time (38:1–12a) and slowing down (38:12b–23). Ponder the ways in which "Clock Management" enhances the story.

BOOK OF ESTHER: Track how the biblical author manages the clock throughout the book, especially in chapters 1 and 4–7. Monitor Esther's decision to approach the king in Esther 4:16, but then track the considerable number of time delays that prevent resolution to this decision, which increases narrative tension and builds more suspense toward the climax in Esther 7.

FOR FURTHER STUDY

Brown, Jeannine K. *The Gospels as Stories: A Narrative Approach to Matthew, Mark, Luke, and John.* Grand Rapids: Baker, 2020. (pp. 40–41)

Licht, Jacob. *Storytelling in the Bible.* Jerusalem: Magnes Press, 1986. (Chapter 5)

Walsh, Jerome T. *Old Testament Narrative: A Guide to Interpretation.* Louisville: Westminster John Knox Press, 2009. (pp. 53–58)

10

Out of Order

SUMMARY: This technique tries to identify when the biblical author arranges events out of the chronological order in which they occurred in real time. The technical term for this is called "chronological displacement," where an author intentionally depicts events in an order that is different from its chronological context. Once these "Out of Order" events are observed, the reader can pinpoint the biblical author's thematic or theological intent for the passage.

PREVALENCE: This device occurs occasionally but frequently enough to warrant investigation. This is only found in narrative books because that genre typically works with a timeline where this can be observed.

INSTRUCTION: While reading, be on the lookout for events that seem out of place or do not fit the timeline. Once they are observed, consider what could have been the author's rationale for moving events from the actual timeline, and think about how this rearranging might reveal the author's thematic or theological goals for the book.

VALUE/PAYOFF: Being aware of when events are out of order provides readers a rich inroad to pondering why the author would have intentionally reordered the timeline to highlight a thematic or theological point.

CHALLENGES: This one is more challenging because it requires that readers have a sense of the overall timeline in which the events described occurred in order to discern when something may be out of chronological order. It also requires them to embrace some degree of subjectivity in pondering why the author chose to place events in the order they are in the text and what the thematic or theological rationale may be for such a move.

EXAMPLES FROM NONBIBLICAL WORKS:

Absalom, Absalom! **by William Faulkner:** Faulkner uses chronological displacement (flashback) to tell the story of Thomas Sutpen. This has the effect of manipulating readers' opinions about individual characters.

Wuthering Heights **by Emily Brontë:** Catherine is already a ghost at the start of the book. The entire story is one long flashback. Nelly Dean rehearses the love story between Heathcliff and Catherine. This has the effect of connoting that time does not limit love.[14]

Lost **(TV show):** This show uses a series of time-manipulated storytelling techniques, including flashbacks, flash-forwards, and simultaneity (where the action is being depicted in different locales at the same time). These techniques add to the "lostness" that characters (and viewers) are experiencing. In one episode, one of the main characters, Jack, goes to Hoffs-Drawlar Funeral Parlor. The name "Hoffs-Drawlar" is an anagram (word formed by rearranging the same letters) that spells "flash-forward." This foreshadows the episode's final scene, when it is revealed that the narrative took place in the future instead of the past.

When I am introduced and asked to share a bit about myself and my testimony of coming to Christ, I do not share my life story in chronological order. I might even start my time mentioning I am married to Gayle and I have two adult children and three grandchildren before I talk about where I was born and raised and the circumstances surrounding how I came to Christ. The genre of a verbal testimony does not require that all the events be shared in chronological order. The story of my life can be topically arranged. I can talk about aspects of my life in groupings—such as my family life, schooling, or career—in a way that is not chronological. Certainly, the facts of my life as I share them are true, but I have the liberty to arrange the events to make for a cohesive presentation around different aspects of my life.

Readers of the Bible sometimes struggle to cope with the fact that what they read in the text is not always given in linear chronological order. However, we have to understand that the Scriptures are not written with our Western journalistic style of writing history. We can't assume that the way we write history today (linear and chronological) is the same way the biblical authors wrote. Biblical authors often rearranged the content around themes or topics instead of a strict linear timeline. When biblical authors write out of chronological order, it is not intended to deceive the reader or rewrite history but rather to shape the storyline with a thematic or theological focus.

A clear example of this is the order of the temptations by Satan of Jesus in the wilderness soon after He was baptized in the Jordan by John the Baptist, as shown by the gospel writers Matthew and Luke:

ORDER OF THE TEMPTATIONS		
	Matthew 4:1–11	Luke 4:1–13
1)	Turn stones into bread	Turn stones into bread
2)	Jump from the pinnacle of the temple	Worship me and I will give you all the kingdoms of the world
3)	Worship me and I will give you all the kingdoms of the world	Jump from the pinnacle of the temple

The order of the second and third temptations are different in these two gospels. Matthew concludes with Satan tempting Jesus to worship him, whereas Luke concludes with Satan tempting Jesus to jump from the temple in Jerusalem. A wrongheaded approach to this variation would be to ask which gospel writer is right in their order (with the assumption that the other is wrong). Instead, recognizing that there is a chronological difference should cause us to slow down and ponder why there is a difference in these two depictions of the same event.

In this instance, an astute reader can see how it is that the order of the temptations fits the overall thematic goal of each author and that a strict chronological timeline is secondary to the author's primary theological purpose for the whole book. It makes thematic sense for Matthew to end with Jesus refusing the offer of Satan for the "kingdoms" of this world because one of the themes of Matthew's gospel is to present Jesus as "King." To conclude with that temptation fits his agenda better.

For Luke, finishing the temptation account with Jesus being tempted to jump from the pinnacle of the temple in Jerusalem fits his thematic purposes, since one of the repeated motifs of Luke's gospel is the city of Jerusalem. In Luke's other work, the book of Acts, the events begin in Jerusalem and then expand out from there in ever widening circles—Jerusalem, Judea, Samaria, to the ends of the earth (see Acts 1:8)—so Jerusalem is a deliberate focus in his writings. In the temptation account, Matthew just mentions the pinnacle of the temple but does not specify its location, whereas Luke spotlights Jerusalem by specifically mentioning it in his account (Luke 4:9).

It is this close attention to detail that can lead to productive insights that point readers to rich personal discovery. Watching how time is arranged in the text deeply enriches our enjoyment of it as we notice features that demonstrate the literary masterpiece that is Scripture and the artful way both the human and divine authors crafted the Word of God to enhance our appreciation of what is contained within its pages.

BIBLICAL EXAMPLES OF "OUT OF ORDER"

Genesis 9–12

Another example of this "Out of Order" phenomenon is found in Genesis 9–12. Once again, the purpose of this is not to try to deceive readers, but rather, to get them to focus on themes and content and not just time sequence.

Genesis 11:1 tells us that the earth at that point had one language. However, in the chapter just prior (which describes what is commonly called the Table of Nations since it lists all the offspring from Noah's sons and where they relocated), the text specifically mentions *languages* (plural) (see Gen. 10:20, 31). It seems rather odd that just two verses later, the author of Genesis mentions that there was only one language (Gen. 11:1)! There is clearly some tension in the chronological order.

Once that tension is recognized, as readers we should pause and consider why the chronological order is not linear. More than likely, the events of chapter 11 (the Tower of Babel and the subsequent scattering) caused the offspring of Noah to spread out (since their languages were confused after the tower incident). This becomes the catalyst for the different "languages" (plural) of Genesis 10.

So why would Moses place the account of the Tower of Babel (the cause) after the Table of Nations (the effect)? Most likely, the order of events was switched for thematic reasons. This chronological displacement helps us understand one of the themes of Genesis, which is that God has a heart for the nations to be blessed (Gen. 12:3), that the nations are a part of His plan. The Table of Nations in Genesis 10 comes right after God's instruction to Noah in Genesis 9 to be "fruitful, multiply and fill the earth" (Gen. 9:1). Therefore, there is a positive aura about the nations in Genesis 10 because they are seen as a fulfillment of the Noahic blessing. If the Table of Nations (Gen. 10) had been placed chronologically (after the Tower of Babel in Genesis 11), then readers would be more likely to see the spreading of the nations in a more negative light since it would have immediately followed and resulted from a sinful and prideful act of rebellion.

Another theological and thematic benefit for the current (nonchronological) order is that we get to see the stark difference between what the men of Babel wanted to do (make their name great—see Gen. 11:4) and what God did (bless one man, Abram, to make His name great—see Gen. 12:2). In contrast to the men of Babel who acted unilaterally, now it is God who chooses who to make "great."

1 and 2 Samuel

Another instance of chronological displacement is in 2 Samuel (chapters 21–24), where events that happened earlier in David's life are included in a section at the end of the book (similar to an appendix in modern-day books) to recount earlier incidents that were skipped over before David passes off the scene. They were not inserted where they occurred on a strict linear timeline because they might have detracted from the author's thematic goals in what he wanted to accomplish in those earlier incidents from his life. Hannah's song (1 Samuel 2) sets up a major theme for the books of Samuel, where God raises up humble leaders and brings down leaders who are proud (see the section in chapter 7, "Poetic Diamonds," for more details). Had these incidents (described at the end of 2 Samuel) been included chronologically, they might have overshadowed that theme. The author still wanted to include them for the record, to portray isolated actions of David to help to characterize the type of person David was, as the record of David's life draws to a close. This section begins and ends with two narrative accounts (2 Sam. 21:1–14 and 2 Sam. 24) that chronicle David's ability to mitigate disaster befalling the Israelite nation as a result of seeking the Lord's face in prayer (2 Sam. 21:1; 24:10, 14).

Psalms

Another clear example of "Out of Order" is in the book of Psalms. The first psalm ever composed, Psalm 90 (which is attributed to Moses), is not inserted at the beginning of the book even though it is the first written psalm chronologically. One likely reason for this chronological displacement is that Psalm 90 serves as a thematic introduction to Book Four of the Psalms (90–106). Scholars have noticed that the book of Psalms consists of 150 poems divided into five books, which are marked off by concluding doxologies (1–41, 42–72, 73–89, 90–106, 107–150), so Psalm 90 was intentionally placed in its current location for reasons other than time of composition.

Observing "Out of Order" events is yet another way we can enjoy Bible reading more. This "chronological displacement" should not diminish our view of the authority of God's Word. When events are out of order, it is not done by biblical authors to minimize the historical truth of what happened but rather to convey theological and thematic purposes. Pay attention to when events are described out of chronological order and look for evidence of the thematic and theological insights that the biblical author has infused into the narrative. Identifying things that are out of order can be a time of joyful discovery as we uncover themes in Scripture and marvel at God's artistry in composing and arranging His Word.

GO and IMPLEMENT

ISAIAH: Reflect on why Isaiah's call to ministry (Isa. 6) occurs after the book has already chronicled some of his prophetic teaching.

JUDGES: Judges 18:30 mentions an individual who could have only lived during the early days of the period of the Judges. Reflect on how this "Out of Order" reference throws into question the view that apostasy was a slow downward spiral in the book.

FOR FURTHER STUDY

Allis, Oswald T. *The Old Testament: Its Claims and Its Critics*. Grand Rapids: Baker, 1972. (pp. 105–10)

Brown, Jeannine K. *The Gospels as Stories: A Narrative Approach to Matthew, Mark, Luke, and John*. Grand Rapids: Baker, 2020. (p. 37)

Licht, Jacob. *Storytelling in the Bible*. Jerusalem: Magnes Press, 1986. (Chapter 5)

Licona, Michael. *Why Are There Differences in the Gospels?: What We Can Learn from Ancient Biography*. Oxford: Oxford University Press, 2016. (Chapter 5)

Ska, Jean Louis. *"Our Fathers Have Told Us": Introduction to the Analysis of Hebrew Narratives*. 2nd ed. Rome: Editrice Pontificio Istituto Biblico, 2000. (pp. 9–12)

Sternberg, Meir. *The Poetics of Biblical Narrative*. Bloomington, IN: Indiana University Press, 1987. (pp. 478–79)

11

You Can Say That Again!

SUMMARY: Repetition is one of the more common literary devices and can take many forms, but it typically involves repeated words, phrases, or other elements to draw the reader's attention or to serve other rhetorical functions.

PREVALENCE: It is prevalent in all sorts of genres. It can range from small units (within verses) to longer passages in repeated episodes and even across multiple texts by different authors.

INSTRUCTION: Pay close attention to when an author uses a word or phrase repeatedly within an account. Identifying repetitions in larger sections requires readers to constantly be on the lookout. When there are side-by-side accounts with repetition, it is good to identify the subtle differences. One of the best ways to catch repetition is to read the text out loud (2 Kings 1–2 is a great example where multiple repeated words and phrases are present). Repetitions of the same word in clusters of seven and ten are relatively common, so count the repeated elements and see if hits one of these benchmarks.

VALUE/PAYOFF: Repeating a word or phrase in a literary work automatically draws attention to itself. Repetition can (1) make a text more memorable and enjoyable, (2) bring cohesion to a text and serve to mark textual boundaries or establish a pattern, (3) highlight a key theme, or (4) slow down the action to allow the reader to reflect on the repeated element more deeply (such as when an author wants the reader to make a comparison or see significant deviations in the repetition).

CHALLENGES: Repetition can be found over large sections or they can be localized. The more repetitions there are within close proximity, the easier they are to see. Repetition that occurs over longer stretches are more challenging to spot. The many different types of repetition (single words, phrases, domains, etc.) can also make them difficult to find. A major hurdle for English Bible readers is that sometimes the repetition is based on original language roots that don't show up in English translations (due to translators using synonyms or the fact that the original language may have two different meanings but use the same root). Readers who wish to overcome this roadblock should read English translations that seek to be more literal in their translation philosophy, such as the New American Standard Bible, which makes it more likely to observe repeated words.

EXAMPLES FROM NONBIBLICAL WORKS:

Abraham Lincoln: "And that government of the people, by the people, for the people, shall not perish from the earth" (Gettysburg Address).

Star Wars films: "I have a bad feeling about this" is a recurring phrase throughout the Star Wars series and is spoken by one of the characters just before something ominous is about to happen.

A Tale of Two Cities by **Charles Dickens:** The first sentence of the novel is full of repetition: "It was the best of times, it was the worst of times, it was the age of wisdom, it was the age of foolishness, it was the epoch of belief, it was the epoch of incredulity, it was the season of Light, it was the season of Darkness, it was the spring of hope, it was the winter of despair. . . ."[15] Dickens uses repetition throughout the novel to highlight themes of fate and contrast.

In aviation, words that are repeated in quick fashion, such as "Mayday, mayday, mayday" or "Eject, eject, eject," are designed to get the attention of those listening and spur immediate action because people's lives are in danger. In this situation, the intent behind the repetition is obvious. Airports and train stations repeatedly broadcast the phrase "If you see something, say something" to prompt passengers to report any suspicious activity and to remind them that they could have a role in preventing an attack.

In my classes at Moody Bible Institute, I often repeat the following phrase: "Let the text set the agenda." This is a reminder to focus on what the biblical author wants to say first before approaching it with questions from our current worldview.

In our world today, repetition is often seen as something negative. Students are told in high school composition classes to vary their words and use synonyms to avoid being repetitive and redundant. Authors from biblical times, however, were under no such restrictions. In fact, repetition characterizes ancient Mesopotamian literature (such as the *Epic of Gilgamesh*) and Greek epic literature (such as Homer). As readers, if we want to enhance our enjoyment of the Bible, rather than viewing repetition negatively we should take advantage of the insights it offers us.

REPETITION IN SCRIPTURE

Repetition in a single verse of Scripture is not only easy to spot but also demonstrates one of the payoffs of observing its presence. For instance, in 1 Corinthians 13:11, Paul states: "When I was a child, I talked like a child, I thought like a child, I reasoned like a child." (The technical term for this literary device is *epistrophe*, which involves repeating a word at the end of every clause or line.) Paul could have avoided the redundancy and said, "When I was a child, I talked, thought, and reasoned like a child," but the rhetorical and poetical force would have been lost, and the point he was making would not have been as memorable.

Frequently, words are used repetitively in a passage to dovetail with what the author is foregrounding on the surface of the text. For example, in describing Solomon's reign, the text of 1 Kings 9:26–10:29 uses the word "gold" fifteen times. This repetition adds rhetorical punch that Solomon's wealth is indeed a central aspect of his kingdom.

Repetition can also occur with a word or phrase repeated in specific multiples. Clusters of seven are very common. Seven is often used in the Scriptures to signify completeness or wholeness, so it makes sense that biblical authors often used that particular number for rhetorical effect and to emphasize a particular theme.

For instance, in the Cain and Abel account in Genesis 4:1–17, the words "brother" and "Abel" are each repeated seven times and "Cain" is repeated fourteen times (a multiple of seven). Cain asks the Lord, "Am I my brother's keeper?" The sevenfold repetition of the word "brother" leaves no doubt to the reader that the answer to that question is yes, even though no direct answer is given in the text.

In this instance, the sevenfold repetitious familial designation ("brother") subtly reveals the practical thrust that the author (Moses) wants his readers to take to heart: that brotherly love toward kin is an essential trait that should characterize us. This is just one example of how identifying repetition can lead to practical application that is anchored in the text. Biblical authors are not just relaying facts about people and events but also seeking to motivate readers to develop godly character.

Now, you may be wondering, if the author wanted to communicate that we should be our "brother's keeper," why didn't he just state that directly instead of leaving it to readers to come to that conclusion based on the use of repetition? For one thing, unlike other genres of Scripture (such as epistles), narrative texts are rarely direct and specific with applications. Authors of narratives use creative, artful, and subtle ways to provide clues as to what readers should focus on and apply. Attentive readers who are aware of these literary devices and the rhetorical thematic value that they provide are on solid footing in drawing applications from the text. Awareness of these devices (such as repetition) helps us stay in sync with the rhythms of the biblical author and follow the promptings of the text rather than subjective hunches about how to apply it.

In Numbers 32, we find even more support that "brotherly love" is a key theme that Moses wants us readers to apply after reading Genesis 4. At the end of Israel's wilderness journey, the tribes of Reuben and Gad approach Moses to request permission to refrain from crossing over the Jordan to conquer Canaan with the rest of tribes, since they are content with the current location in the Transjordan region. In Numbers 32:6, Moses responds to their request: "But Moses said to the people of Gad and to the people of Reuben, 'Shall your *brothers* go to the war while you sit here?'"

In Genesis, Moses began the story arc of human existence after the fall with an account of a brother failing his sibling, and in Numbers, Moses ends this story arc with another incident where brothers were seeking to circumvent their brotherly obligations yet again. Astute readers of the Pentateuch should deduce that this is an intentional applicational thrust. The sevenfold repetition of "brother" in Genesis 4:1–17 (which seems redundant since it is already known information to readers) is further evidence supporting that theme.

Another example of sevenfold repetition occurs in the book of Ephesians. In Ephesians 4:4–6, the word "one" is repeated seven times. This sevenfold repetition of "one" dovetails with one of Paul's thematic purposes for the entire book, which is unity.

Occasionally, sevenfold repetitions of phrases occur over an entire book. For instance, in the gospel of John, the phrase "these things I have spoken to you" (or "I have said these things to you") appears seven times in the book (John 14:25; 15:11; 16:1, 4, 6, 25, 33). The fact that these clusters are strategic (either structural or thematically) seems to indicate that they are intentional and purposeful.

Specialized Occurrences of Repetitions

Sometimes authors incorporate more specialized uses of repetition to get the reader's attention.

Twofold Repetition of a Proper Name

Be on the lookout for when a proper name is repeated one after the other. Certainly, the addition of the second use of the proper name is redundant since the addressee is already identified. Therefore, it serves a rhetorical purpose when it occurs, which is worthy of investigation.

DUPLICATION OF A PROPER NAME	
Text	**Proper Name**
Gen. 22:11	Abraham, Abraham
Gen. 46:2	Jacob, Jacob
Ex. 3:4	Moses, Moses
1 Sam. 3:10	Samuel, Samuel
Matt. 7:21	Lord, Lord
Luke 10:41	Martha, Martha
Luke 13:34	Jerusalem, Jerusalem
Luke 22:31	Simon, Simon
Acts 9:4	Saul, Saul

These repetitions of proper names occur in contexts where there are strong emotions, a high degree of familiarity between the one speaking and the one hearing, or in theophanies when God makes a personal appearance to an individual.

Repetition with Slight Variations

Not only is it important to look for repetitions, it is also helpful to be on the lookout for variation within repeated passages. Readers might have the tendency to skip over a character's speech if it is repeated by the author. A great example of this is to compare and contrast the different alibis that Potiphar's wife gives in Genesis 39 regarding what Joseph supposedly did to her. The two alibis essentially repeat the same details, but there are very subtle and important variations (first to the household and then to her husband) regarding Joseph's actions. Even though there are many repeated elements between the two, the subtle variation reveals her character.

DIFFERENT ALIBIS OF POTIPHAR'S WIFE	
Alibi to the servants of the household	Alibi to her husband
"See, he has brought among us a Hebrew to laugh at us. He came in to me to lie with me, and I cried out with a loud voice. And as soon as he heard that I lifted up my voice and cried out, he left his garment beside me and fled and got out of the house" (39:14–15).	"The Hebrew servant, whom you have brought among us, came in to me to laugh at me. But as soon as I lifted up my voice and cried, he left his garment beside me and fled out of the house" (39:17–18).

While her speech is nearly identical, both times the variations are what reveal her character. Notice she adds the label "servant" when conversing with her husband, but she only mentions his ethnicity (Hebrew) when talking to the household servants because mentioning Joseph's "servant" status is unlikely to influence them to be sympathetic to her plight (since that is their lot in life as well). She mentions Joseph's Hebrew ethnicity to the household staff to highlight Joseph's "otherness" and build sympathy for an "us versus him" situation. Also, notice the variation between "laugh at us" and "laugh at me," since she knows her husband would not care as much about how the staff interacts with each other, but he would care about how the household servants treat his wife.

This chapter has just scratched the surface of what is involved with repetition. While repetition is a frequent tool that authors use to draw the attention of the reader, we are not explicitly told why that repetition is used. It is up to the reader to actively ponder why the author uses repetition and how it may help to advance the author's themes and purposes for the text.

This is why it is a fresh way for us to enjoy our Bible—it seeks to engage us to actively enter into a dialogue with the text that will yield fresh insights from Scripture. As I constantly remind my students: "Let the text set the agenda." If you pay attention to when repetition is present in your Bible, it will not only give you a deeper understanding of what the author is highlighting but also bring deeper joy as you discover the wonderful intricacies of God's Word.

GO and IMPLEMENT

- Look at how the word "hand" is used in the Joseph narrative, especially in Genesis 37 and 39. Compare and contrast the instances of Joseph's "hands" with other people's "hands."

- Look for the repetition of "all" in Joshua 21:41–43.

- Read John 6:47–59 and look for several repeated words and how those repetitions capture the main theological point of the passage.

FOR FURTHER STUDY

Alter, R. *The Art of Biblical Narrative.* 2nd ed. New York: Basic Books, 2011. (Chapter 5)

Licht, Jacob. *Storytelling in the Bible.* Jerusalem: Magnes Press, 1986. (Chapter 3)

Sternberg, Meir. *The Poetics of Biblical Narrative.* Bloomington: Indiana University Press, 1987. (Chapter 11)

Walsh, Jerome T. *Old Testament Narrative: A Guide to Interpretation.* Louisville: Westminster John Knox, 2009. (Chapter 8)

———. *Style and Structure in Biblical Hebrew Narrative.* Collegeville, MN: Liturgical Press, 2001. (Chapter 8)

12

X Marks the Spot

SUMMARY: Biblical authors often shaped their content in structural ways that are different than what modern readers are accustomed to. One way that biblical writers organized their material was to repeat words, phrases, or concepts inversely around a center in order to shape the overall structure of books, sections, episodes, speeches, or even individual verses. This technique, known as *chiasm*, is based on the Greek letter *chi*, which looks like the letter X in the Greek alphabet. Among scholars there has been a growing awareness that biblical authors use chiasm ("X Marks the Spot") within the Bible. This technique is also known by other names such as concentric parallelism, ring pattern, mirror pattern, and envelope structure. The reason for the label "X Marks the Spot" is two-fold: Firstly, the letter X represents the shape of this literary device in that you have two inverse symmetrical patterns that pivot around a center point. Secondly, the center of this technique often marks a significant thematic point that the author is stressing, much like the X on a treasure map identifies where the riches are located. This structure is similar to "Beautiful Bookends" discussed in chapter 5, but that technique focuses on just the beginnings and endings of texts.

PREVALENCE: It is very common, especially in narrative and poetic texts, but it is also present in the epistles and prophetic books.

INSTRUCTION: Pay close attention to words or phrases that are repeated in close proximity to each other, and then expand outward to see other repeated words, phrases, or concepts. It might be helpful to search online to see if somebody else has observed a chiasm in the text you are studying, and then judge for yourself how strong a case can be made for its presence.

VALUE/PAYOFF: This is a valuable technique in that it signals the coherence of a text in an artful way. Once the center is identified, it can help to underscore a theme that the author is emphasizing or to identify a pivotal event in the account.

CHALLENGES: "X Marks the Spot" or chiastic structures are more evident the more lexical they are, where exact words or phrases are repeated verbatim on each side of the pivot. They are less evident when the elements are more conceptual. There is debate about whether or not there has to be a single center (A, B, C, B', A') or if there can be a doubled center (A, B, C, C', B', A'), which some call "concentric," but the two patterns function the same around the center.

EXAMPLES FROM NONBIBLICAL WORKS:

This device was used in ancient times as well as by modern authors and filmmakers. For instance, the Greek philosopher Socrates is attributed with saying, "Bad men live that they may eat and drink, whereas good men eat and drink that they may live."[16] At his inaugural address, President John F. Kennedy said, "Ask not what your country can do for you; ask what you can do for your country." One of the reasons why that line is so memorable is the chiastic structure.

Beowulf employs this structure, as well as Homer's *Iliad*, so it is a well-established literary technique.[17]

Films such as Disney's animated *Beauty and the Beast*, *Braveheart* by Mel Gibson, and many iterations of the *Spiderman* movies use this technique.[18]

In nearly every home kitchen, there are three major work areas: food storage (refrigerator/freezer), preparation (sink), and cooking (stove/oven). Designers who determine the layout of those three work spaces implement what is referred to as the "work triangle." It is a concept used to determine an efficient kitchen layout that is both functional but also aesthetically gratifying, especially in households where one person does most of the cooking. In such a layout, the kitchen sink anchors the room and is typically in the center of the triangle and equidistant to the other two working areas.

In like manner, biblical authors often anchored their content around a literary centering device known as a chiasm. You may not always be cognizant of the structure, but just like your kitchens are designed around implementing the "work triangle" anchored around the sink, so biblical authors utilized a functional and aesthetically pleasing literary device centering around a pivot that oftentimes reflects a key theme. One clear way to enjoy your Bible on a deeper level is to not only notice this device's presence but to ponder how the pivot anchors the text.

BIBLICAL EXAMPLES OF CHIASTIC STRUCTURES

Genesis 11 (Tower of Babel)

The pivot of the Babel account ("H") and the turning point of the passage is the Lord's coming down to see what the men are building (Gen. 11:5). Notice that this is the center of the passage, and the other elements radiate to and from that event. Why is this the center? Because it is not only the hinge of the account, but it also thematically touches on a major theme of the book of Genesis, which is that God takes the time to personally investigate people's actions before pronouncing judgment. He did that in the garden (Gen. 3:8–9), and He does so again in the Sodom and Gomorrah account using the same "going down" language (Gen. 18:20–21). This repeated theme in Genesis regarding God's character emphasizes that He is patient and does not mete out justice in an arbitrary fashion.

A. "the whole earth" (v. 1)
  B. "had one language and the same words" (v. 1)
    C. "land of Shinar" (v. 2)
      D. "there" (v. 2)
        E. "to one another" (v. 3)
          F. "Come, let us make bricks" (v. 3)
            G. "a city and a tower" (v. 4)
              H. "And the LORD came down to see" (v. 5)
            G'. "the city and the tower" (v. 5)
          F'. "Come, let us go down" (v. 7)
        E'. "may not understand one another's speech" (v. 7)
      D'. "there" (v. 9)
    C'. "Babel" (v. 9)
  B'. "the language of all the earth" (v. 9)
A'. "face of all the earth" (v. 9)

Elsewhere the Scriptures extol God's omniscience (e.g., 1 John 3:20), but in the book of Genesis, the author is introducing the most important character in all the Bible to readers. So, throughout this book he includes accounts that show God in anthropomorphic language, personally investigating situations to see if rebellion is present. He does this with Adam (4:8–9), Babel (11:5), and Sodom (18:20–21). Once God verifies, then He executes justice. The purpose of portraying God in this way is to demonstrate to the reader that God is not capricious (like surrounding ancient Near Eastern gods were depicted) but loving and careful to verify rebellion before administering justice.

Galatians 5

This chapter includes the familiar "fruit of the Spirit" passage, but what readers may not recognize is that verses 22–23 (NASB) are embedded in a larger chiastic structure.

15 But if you bite and devour **one another**, take care that you are not consumed by **one another**.

16 But I say, **walk by the Spirit**, and you will not carry out the desire of the **flesh**.

17 For the **flesh** sets its desire against the Spirit, and the Spirit against the flesh; for these are in opposition to one another, so that you may not do the things that you please.

18 But if you are led by the Spirit, you are **not under the Law**.

19 Now the **deeds of the flesh** are evident, which are: immorality, impurity, sensuality,

20 idolatry, sorcery, enmities, strife, jealousy, outbursts of anger, disputes, dissensions, factions,

21 envying, drunkenness, carousing, and things like these, of which I forewarn you, just as I have forewarned you, that those who practice such things will not inherit the kingdom of God.

22 But the **fruit of the Spirit** is love, joy, peace, patience, kindness, goodness, faithfulness,

23 gentleness, self-control; against such things **there is no law**.

24 Now those who belong to Christ Jesus have crucified the **flesh** with its passions and desires.

25 If we live by the Spirit, let us also **walk by the Spirit**.

26 Let us not become boastful, challenging **one another**, envying **one another**.

By isolating the repeated elements, the overall chiastic structure of Galatians 5 becomes evident.

A. But if you bite and devour **one another**, take care that you are not consumed by **one another**.

  B. But I say, **walk by the Spirit**,

    C. and you will not carry out the desire of the **flesh**.

      D. But if you are led by the Spirit, you are **not under the Law**.

        E. Now the **deeds of the flesh** are evident, which are . . .

        E'. But the **fruit of the Spirit** is . . .

      D'. against such things **there is no law**.

    C'. Now those who belong to Christ Jesus have crucified the **flesh**

  B'. If we live by the Spirit, let us also **walk by the Spirit**.

A'. Let us not become boastful, challenging **one another**, envying **one another**.

Most readers tend to gravitate to the "fruit of the Spirit" (vv. 22–23) verses by default, and this chiastic structure confirms that is indeed the focus of this paragraph since it is at the center. In addition to focusing on the center, the reader can profit as well by looking at the content at the beginning and end of the "X" structure (5:15, 26) and see how that content "frames" the discussion. By doing so with this passage, a very practical takeaway becomes evident: the fruit of the Spirit is best manifested not in isolation but in community with other believers where verbal bickering is not present. Lack of strife is, therefore, a key indicator that demonstrates whether or not believers are walking by the Spirit.

Here we see a practical implication of noticing the chiastic structure in this section of Galatians 5. Paul is not simply directing readers to cultivate this fruit in their own individual lives. Rather, he uses this list of qualities (in relation to interaction with other believers) as a barometer to demonstrate whether or not one is walking by the Spirit. For example, I know I am truly walking by the Spirit in my interaction with my wife, Gayle, when the fruit of the Spirit is present and I am loving, patient, gentle, etc. toward her, but if I am not walking by the Spirit, I can be sarcastic and passive-aggressive. This signals to me I need to "crucify my flesh" and instead be carried along by the Spirit's prompting and power rather than my own selfish desires.

Because chiasms are intentionally used by the authors to organize the content of biblical texts, they provide productive insights for readers with almost immediate payoff. By spending focused time on the pivotal sections of these structures, Bible readers are bound to see significant theological, thematic, or practical takeaways and enhance their enjoyment of Scripture once the artistry is observed.

GO and IMPLEMENT

Readers are more likely to identify chiasms in more literal translations (like the New American Standard Bible) because they tend to translate original language words with the same English glosses, which makes it easier to catch repetitions.

JOSHUA 1: Readers are often inspired by Joshua 1:8, but zoom out from that verse to the surrounding verses (1:5–9) and look for the repeated elements that bracket off the middle and how they help to define that pivotal verse. The structure here is not perfectly symmetrical, but take a close look at one of the brackets (which is not in the expected order) and ponder why that is intentional.

ECCLESIASTES 11–12: Look for the chiastic structure in Ecclesiastes 11:3–12:2 and take notice that this structure even crosses chapter boundaries.

PSALMS: Many psalms utilize this structure. Identify its usage in Psalms 18 and 25.

FOR FURTHER STUDY

Deppe, Dean B. *All Roads Lead to the Text: Eight Methods of Inquiry into the Bible.* Grand Rapids: Eerdmans, 2011. (pp. 25–28; 354–60)

Dorsey, David A. *The Literary Structure of the Old Testament.* Grand Rapids: Baker, 1999.

Erickson, Richard J. *A Beginner's Guide to New Testament Exegesis: Taking the Fear out of Critical Method.* Downers Grove, IL: InterVarsity Press, 2005. (pp. 82–85)

Parks, Ward. "Ring Structure and Narrative Embedding in Homer and 'Beowulf.'" *Neuphilologische Mitteilungen* (1988): 237–51.

Walsh, Jerome T. *Old Testament Narrative: A Guide to Interpretation.* Louisville: Westminster John Knox, 2009. (Chapter 10)

13

Heads Up

SUMMARY: "Heads Up" or foreshadowing is a device authors use to arrange events or information in order to prepare the reader for later material. They are dropped or mentioned in seminal form and authors do not announce their presence or purpose explicitly. These mentions not only prepare the reader for later developments but also build anticipation. They foreshadow significant elements of the plot or a theme that the author is foregrounding.

PREVALENCE: They appear more often than readers might think, but they are not necessarily present in every book of the Bible.

INSTRUCTION: Foreshadowing can be incorporated into a text in several different ways, so it requires focused attention and knowledge of the broader context to perceive it. Familiarity with the ways authors signal its presence is probably the best place that readers can start to find foreshadowing. Authors often hint at foreshadowing by embedding this technique in a character's direct speech, inserting an element or an object in the setting that will be instrumental later, or describing actions that will be mirrored later in the account.

VALUE/PAYOFF: It primes the reader, and builds anticipation and suspense. Hint dropping can be helpful for providing clues about what may happen in the future, revealing character traits, or setting up the reader emotionally for plot twists.

CHALLENGES: The big challenge is that foreshadowing can typically only be recognized as such "after the fact," when readers have additional information to help contextualize people and events and make sense of what was mentioned earlier. This requires repeated and focused reading skills.

EXAMPLES FROM NONBIBLICAL WORKS:

Frankenstein (nineteenth-century novel by Mary Shelley): When Victor was young, two events foreshadow his future: 1) exposure to mystical treatises that don't respect the boundaries and limitations of modern science, and 2) a violent thunderstorm where he learns about electricity. He will later go on to transgress the boundaries of the possible by learning to reanimate dead matter by electricity.

Many detective or whodunit dramas: These works often utilize foreshadowing so that the "reveal" at the end is not something pulled out of thin air.

Star Wars movies: Whenever a character (e.g., Han Solo) states "I have a bad feeling about this," it is indeed a warning that something bad is about to happen. Obi-Wan says to Anakin, "Why do I get the feeling you will be the death of me?" Indeed, it is Anakin who kills him.

Skyfall (2012 James Bond film): The opening credits are a montage of images: Bond sinking in water, a cemetery, knives, guns, a skull, and Chinese dragons. Each image foreshadows characters, scenes, and objects that are central in the film.

In many situations, people enjoy getting a heads up to alert or prepare them for something. Employees like to be tipped off in advance that their boss may be in a foul mood that day so they can avoid aggravating him or her. Students like to be given a heads up about an impending pop quiz that the teacher plans to give in class. Shoppers like to know in advance about upcoming sales.

Yet at the same time, many people go to great lengths to avoid hearing any information about films or TV show episodes they have not seen yet or the scores of games they missed watching live. However, there is research that suggests that revealing or hinting at a story's ending in advance may actually increase enjoyment![19] One rationale for this is "processing fluency"—even after getting a heads up or being exposed to a hint or a spoiler, the upcoming contents of the story are anticipated, easing the reader/viewer's ability to process and comprehend the different elements of the account. This makes the experience enjoyable for many even if they have actively tried to avoid spoilers and were unsuccessful.

The researchers also found that "heads ups" provide "pleasurable tension." Knowing ahead of time about a plot twist or a major reveal increases a reader's elation and draws more attention to how the characters respond to the tension created by the author's depiction of events.

Just because you know the outcome in advance does not mean that reading (or rewatching) something is not enjoyable. Foreshadowing in Scripture actually enhances our reading experience as it helps us to be more active readers and look for all the ways that details of the account correspond to the already known outcome. We all know people who read the same book over and over or watch the same film a number of times. Similarly, as Bible readers, even though we already know the ending (God wins!), we can still enjoy the ride repeatedly.

EXAMPLES OF FORESHADOWING IN SCRIPTURE

Some Bible books contain what are more traditional "spoiler alerts," such as when Genesis 13:10 mentions the destruction of Sodom and Gomorrah before it is described in Genesis 19, or when John mentions Judas in John 12:4 as the one who would betray Jesus before it happens (John 13:21–30). These examples are relatively rare and are fairly obvious to spot. In this chapter we are focusing on the more subtle "Heads Up" cases where authors mention things that artfully signal events that will come to pass later.

Authors can intentionally select certain details of an earlier event that will be matched in a later incident to help prep the reader for those events and to foreground certain themes or aspects that they want to be more prominent in their writing. Scholars sometimes mention cases of foreshadowing that occur across different books (intertextual), but this chapter will focus on intra-textual examples that are within the confines of a single book as they will be easier for readers to detect because of the narrower context.

A good example of this technique is in the gospel of Matthew, where events in the birth narrative of Jesus foreshadow events in His passion (death) narrative, such as when Matthew mentions:

- **Religious leaders' apathy and antagonism to Christ:** The anguished meeting of the chief priests and teachers of the law when Herod asks them about where the Messiah was to be born (2:4) portends a later incident when the chief priests and other religious leaders conspire to seek Jesus' death (26:3–5).

- **Threatening political authorities**[20]: King Herod in 2:1–12 mirrors Pilate in 27:11–26. Not only do Herod's actions foreshadow the future but they also echo a previous ruler's response to God's premier act of redemption in the Old Testament by mirroring Pharaoh's slaughtering of Hebrew boys prior to the exodus (Ex. 2).

- **The title "King of the Jews":** The wise men journeying to seek the "king of Jews" (2:2) foreshadows Pilate asking Jesus if He is the "King of the Jews" (27:11), the soldiers deriding Jesus using that title (27:29), and the message they placed over Jesus' head on the cross (27:37).[21]

• **Including the Gentiles in God's purposes:** The early mentions of Gentiles (1:1, 5–6; 2:1–12; 4:12–16; 8:5–13) and their inclusion anticipates the final command of Christ to make disciples of all nations (28:16–20).[22]

• **Worship:** The worship of Jesus by "wise men from the east" (Matt. 2:1) is matched by the Eleven worshiping Jesus after His resurrection (28:17).

Notice how this foreshadowing not only helps prep the reader for later events but also highlights themes that Matthew wants his readers to incorporate into their own lives as they engage his account of Jesus. Astute readers will be in step with Matthew's authorial intentions on a practical level when they personally seek tangible ways in their own lives to extend Christ's mission to the Gentiles and when they worship Him.

Genesis

Another example of foreshadowing occurs in Genesis 12. John Sailhamer notes the similarities between Abraham's visit in Egypt with that of the Israelites' sojourn in the same place. Genesis 12 shows how Abram's actions in Egypt clearly foreshadow what will happen to the sons of Jacob in that same place. The earlier account prepares the reader and points the way to what will happen later.

SIMILARITIES BETWEEN ABRAM IN EGYPT AND ISRAELITE SOJOURN IN EGYPT[23]	
Genesis 12–13	**Genesis 41–Exodus 12**
"There was a famine in the land" (12:10)	"There was famine in all lands" (41:54)
"When he was about to enter Egypt" (12:11)	"they came into the land of Goshen" (46:28)
"he said to Sarai his wife" (12:11)	"Joseph said to his brothers" (46:31)
"I know that . . ." (12:11)	"I will go up and tell Pharaoh . . ." (46:31)
"and when the Egyptians see you, they will say . . ." (12:12)	"When Pharaoh calls you and says . . ." (46:33)
"Say . . ." (12:13)	"Say . . ." (46:34)
"that it may go well with me because of you" (12:13)	"that you may dwell in the land of Goshen" (46:34)
"And when the princes of Pharaoh saw her, they praised her to Pharaoh" (12:15)	"So Joseph went in and told Pharaoh . . ." (47:1)
"And the woman was taken into Pharaoh's house" (12:15)	"Then Pharaoh said . . . 'Settle your father and your brothers in the best of the land'" (47:5)
"Abram . . . had sheep, oxen, male donkeys" (12:16)	"Put them in charge of my livestock" (47:6) "they gained possessions in it, and were fruitful and multiplied greatly" (47:27)
"But the LORD afflicted Pharaoh and his house with great plagues" (12:17)	"Yet one plague more I will bring upon Pharaoh" (Ex. 11:1)
"So Pharaoh called Abram and said . . ." (12:18)	"Then he [Pharaoh] summoned Moses and Aaron by night and said . . ." (12:31)
"take . . . and go" (12:19)	"Take . . . and be gone" (12:32)
"and they sent him away" (12:20)	"to send them out of the land" (12:33)
"So Abram went up from Egypt . . . into the Negeb" (13:1)	"And the people of Israel journeyed from Rameses to Succoth" (12:37)
"and Lot went with him" (13:1)	"A mixed multitude also went up with them" (12:38)
"Now Abram was very rich in livestock, in silver, and in gold" (13:2)	"and very much livestock" (12:38) "silver and gold" (12:35)

Judges

Samson's line in Judges 14:2 ("Then he came up and told his father and mother, 'I saw one of the daughters of the Philistines at Timnah. Now get her for me as my wife'") serves as a foreshadowing device as Samson's problematic "seeing" will come up again and again (14:7, 8; 16:1, 21, 28). Samson's spiritual blindness and doing "what is right in his own eyes" ultimately leads to his physical blindness, and all of this is set in motion by the "Heads Up" alert in 14:2.

Foreshadowing is a creative literary device implemented by biblical authors to help mentally and emotionally prepare readers for later content. In addition, once it is detected after the fact, it provides readers with a real sense of joyous accomplishment for having recognized its presence (a biblical "eureka!" moment). This is a fresh way to increase your reading pleasure while engaging God's eternal Word.

GO and IMPLEMENT

Luke does the same thing that Matthew does by using details from Jesus' birth narrative to foreshadow His death and resurrection. Investigate and try to discover some examples.

Investigate Solomon's prayer at the dedication of the temple and the LORD's response (1 Kings 8–9), and look for ways that prayer foreshadows elements of the Babylonian exile and Solomon's downfall later in the corpus of 1–2 Kings.

The creation account has many commonalities with the flood narrative. Look for the repeated elements between Genesis 1 and Genesis 7–9 and see how these "Heads Up" alerts help readers to view Noah as a new Adam-like figure in a "do over" account.

FOR FURTHER STUDY

Sailhamer, John. *Introduction to Old Testament Theology: A Canonical Approach.* Grand Rapids: Zondervan, 1995. (pp. 294–95)

Sternberg, Meir. *The Poetics of Biblical Narrative.* Bloomington: Indiana University Press, 1987.

Walsh, Jerome T. *Old Testament Narrative: A Guide to Interpretation.* Louisville: Westminster John Knox, 2009. (pp. 59–62)

Déjà Vu

SUMMARY: The label for the technique described in this chapter will be "Déjà Vu" (from the French "already seen"), which is a technique where biblical authors mirror events or people with later events or people paralleling and matching them by using the same or similar details.

PREVALENCE: Typically this is found in narrative books because it is built on people and events.

INSTRUCTION: Pay close attention to similarities of accounts or people that are mirrored or echoed in other accounts. As you read later texts, pause and reflect on whether the content sounds similar to the content of earlier people or events. Look for connections that are either lexical or thematic.

VALUE/PAYOFF: This technique is important because it clearly demonstrates how interconnected the stories of the Bible are. Many times, accounts have similar elements that give the reader a déjà vu experience as they read through the narrative. Readers of the Bible often approach the text in a linear fashion, but many of the stories are meant to be read cyclically. Identifying these cyclical events helps readers to see themes and similarities between events and characters that the author wants us to see.

CHALLENGES: If the echo is closer in proximity, then they are more readily detectable. Echoes that occur farther apart are more challenging to detect. Sometimes characters mirror each other, and if they are prominent characters described in greater detail, there is more likelihood to see the linkage.

EXAMPLES FROM NONBIBLICAL WORKS:

Hamlet by William Shakespeare: Deaths of three fathers lead to a mission of revenge by their respective sons (Hamlet, Laertes, and Fortinbras). Hamlet and Laertes really parallel one another: both grew up in the royal court, both have a relationship with Ophelia, both are scholars, and both are able swordsman who respected their fathers deeply.

Star Wars films: There are many parallels between characters and between films. For instance, Padme and Leia are mother and daughter, and even though they are separated at birth, they share parallel experiences: both are royalty, both served in the senate, both are selfless, and both seek to understand who they are. Whole films mirror each other. For instance, episodes two and five (middle films of their respective trilogies) contain parallel situations: both inject a love interest (Anakin/Padme and Han/Leia), both feature flying into asteroid fields, both feature a dismantling of C-3PO, and both depict a Skywalker losing a hand (Anakin/Luke).

In life there are many repeatable cycles, such as the four seasons or the sun rising and setting every day. The same can be true in literature. Accounts sometimes have similar events to previous ones, which in turn establishes a pattern or theme. Sometimes what one character experiences is matched by similar events in another character's life later on.

This does not signal that the accounts are fictional. Out of all the details available, biblical authors selected specific situations that mirror what happened earlier for thematic purposes. Biblical authors are not lazy or unoriginal when they do this, but it is intentionally done to invite the reader to look for similarities and differences or to make their account enjoyable for the reader once they catch what is going on. It actually speaks to the care and artistry that biblical authors went through under the inspiration process (see 2 Tim. 3:16; 2 Peter 1:21).

The Scriptures are not just a depository of information but artfully designed revelation that reflects the creative abilities of the sovereign God of the universe, who infused beauty and design not just in the world that He created but also the Word of God that He composed.

There are other names for these types of connections, such as *parallel structure / extended echo* ("similarity of structure in a pair or series of related words, phrases, or clauses"[24]), *intertextuality* (similarity across books) or *intra-textuality* (similarity within a book), where one text echoes what was communicated in an earlier text, and *recursion*, where an author deliberately shapes a narrative so that elements of one account are repeated in another account.[25] (For an example of recursion, see the chart comparing Abram's actions with those of Israel in chapter 13.)

Intra-Textual Examples of "Déjà Vu" in Scripture

PARALLELS BETWEEN ADAM AND CAIN IN GENESIS 3–4		
Similarity	**Adam (3:9–18)**	**Cain (4:9–16)**
Question Asked	"Where are you?"	"Where is Abel . . . ?"
Retort Given	"The woman whom you gave to be with me . . ."	"Am I my brother's keeper?"
Follow-Up Question	"What is this that you have done?"	"What have you done?"
Curse Statement	"Cursed is the ground . . ."	"You are cursed from the ground . . ."
Provision	Animal skins	Mark of Cain

Clearly there is an echo of Genesis 3 in Genesis 4, and once readers "hear" that echo and experience a bit of déjà vu, they can begin to ponder why such parallels exist between the two accounts. In these texts, it is apparent that the adage "like father, like son" applies.

John Sailhamer has identified another clear example of this in the mirroring of the creation and flood accounts in Genesis.

PARALLELS BETWEEN CREATION AND FLOOD ACCOUNTS[26]		
	Creation Account	**Flood Account**
1.	"and darkness was over the face of the deep" (1:2)	"all the fountains of the great deep burst forth" (7:11)
2.	"and let the dry land appear" (1:9)	"the tops of the mountains were seen" (8:5)
3.	"Let the earth sprout vegetation" (1:11–12)	"in her mouth was a freshly plucked olive leaf" (8:11)
4.	"let them be for signs and for seasons, and for days and years" (1:14)	"in the first month, the first day of the month" (8:13)
5.	"And God said, 'Let the land bring forth living creatures'" (1:24)	"Then God said . . . 'Bring out with you every living thing'" (8:15, 17)

6.	"And God blessed them, saying, 'Be fruitful and multiply and fill the waters'" (1:22)	"Then God said . . . 'be fruitful and multiply on the earth'" (8:15, 17)
7.	"Let us make man" (1:26)	"So Noah went out" (8:18)
8.	"And God blessed them. And God said to them, "Be fruitful and multiply and fill the earth" (1:28)	"And God blessed Noah and his sons and said to them, 'Be fruitful and multiply and fill the land'" (9:1)
9.	"have dominion over the fish of the sea" (1:28b)	". . . and all the fish of the sea. Into your hand they are delivered" (9:2)
10.	"And God said, 'Behold, I have given you . . . for food'" (1:29)	"shall be for food for you" (9:3)

The reason why the flood account is a "Déjà Vu" experience for the reader is that Moses intends for the reader to view Noah as an Adam-like figure and the flood as an example of God mercifully allowing a do-over of the creation account. Sadly, however, Noah is not much different from Adam as the text goes on to give more "Déjà Vu" experiences for the reader between Adam and Noah.

ADAM/EVE (GENESIS 2–3)	NOAH (GENESIS 9:20–27)[27]
"And the LORD God planted a garden . . . and there he put the man" (2:8)	"Noah . . . planted a vineyard." (9:20)
"she took of [the tree] and ate" (3:6)	"He drank of the wine and became drunk" (9:21)
"and they knew that they were naked." (3:7a)	"and [he] lay uncovered in his tent" (9:21)
"And they sewed fig leaves together and made themselves loincloths." (3:7b)	"[They] covered the nakedness of their father." (9:23)
"Then the eyes of both were opened, and they knew that they were naked." (3:7a)	"When Noah awoke from his wine and knew what his youngest son had done to him" (9:24)
"cursed are you" (3:14)	"Cursed be Canaan" (9:25)

Even more intriguing is another "Déjà Vu" parallel between Noah and Lot. Readers would not normally see them in parallel, but the lexical connections are numerous and hard to ignore.

PARALLELS BETWEEN NOAH AND LOT		
Similarity	Noah	Lot
Described as "righteous"	"Noah was a **righteous** man" (Gen. 6:9; see also 7:1; Heb. 11:7)	"Will you indeed sweep away the **righteous** with the wicked?" (Gen. 18:23; see also 2 Peter 2:6–9)
Same verb ("destroy")	"I will **destroy** them with the earth." (6:13)	"For we are about to **destroy** this place, because the outcry against its people has become great before the LORD, and the LORD has sent us to **destroy** it." (19:13; see also 18:28; 19:14)
Family saved	"Go into the ark, you and all your household" (7:1)	"Then the men said to Lot, 'Have you anyone else here? Sons-in-law, sons, daughters, or anyone you have in the city, bring them out of the place.'" (19:12)
Elemental force wipes out humanity	"For in seven days I will send **rain** [Heb. *matar*] on the earth forty days and forty nights." (7:4) "And **rain** fell upon the earth forty days and forty nights." (7:12)	"the LORD **rained** [Heb. *matar*] on Sodom and Gomorrah **sulfur and fire** from the LORD out of heaven." (19:24)
Door shut to keep out the wicked	"And those that entered, male and female of all flesh, went in as God had commanded him. And the LORD **shut** him in." (7:16)	"But the men reached out their hands and brought Lot into the house with them and **shut** the door." (19:10)
Drunkenness (only twice mentioned in Genesis)	"He drank of the wine and became drunk." (9:21)	"So they made their father drink wine that night." (19:33)

Sexual impropriety hinted at or performed	"Noah . . . knew what his youngest son had done to him" (9:22–24)	"And the firstborn went in and lay with her father. He did not know when she lay down or when she arose." (19:33) "Thus both the daughters of Lot became pregnant by their father." (19:36)
Children that descend become nations	Shem, Ham, and Japheth (10:1)	Ammon and Moab (19:37–38)
Future nations that trouble Israel	Canaan	Moab and Ammon
Destruction is foretold by God	"And God said to Noah, 'I have determined to make an end of all flesh, for the earth is filled with violence through them. Behold, I will destroy them with the earth.'" (6:13)	"Then the LORD said, 'Because the outcry against Sodom and Gomorrah is great and their sin is very grave'" (18:20)
Saved by two	Shem and Japheth cover their father (9:23)	Two messengers brought Lot inside (19:1, 10)
Water	The earth is flooded with water	Sodom is "well watered" (13:10)
Protection from the world in a structure	Noah in an ark	Lot in a house

This "Déjà Vu" example is good to ponder because left to our own devices we would not think to put those two characters side by side or think that they have so many similarities between them. The author, by paralleling Noah with Adam and then Lot with Noah, is stressing that as humanity goes forward, they still have the same generational sin issues.

What's more is that the consequences of their actions do not result in blessing the nations as God intended but instead bring curses on neighboring nations—the Canaanites (Gen. 9:25) and the Ammonites and Moabites (Deut. 23:3–6). Things are not going in the right direction!

Prior to my conversion to Christ, I had a rocky relationship with my father. In my mind I was going to be my own person, and I certainly did not want to be anything like him when I grew up. Things were still rough for a while even after I came to faith in Jesus, but thankfully the relationship was fully restored before he passed away.

Now as I get older, I have come to realize more and more how my life mirrors that of my father's. The stubbornness and self-ishness that chafed me while I was under my father's roof crops up from time to time in my life, much to my dismay. My father would go to libraries, research obscure topics, and file away lots of documents—which is something I do as well! He networked with many people and was highly determined to get projects to completion, and I have that tendency today. My life mirrors that of my father's, in his good traits and the bad.

Similarly, in the Scriptures there are many characters who mirror each other, which gives us the opportunity to compare and contrast the connecting points of these "Déjà Vu" characters and events. These parallels allow us to see the beautiful grand tapestry of the themes interwoven into the pages of God's Word and delight once again in the towering majesty of the intricate beauty and design of our sacred Scriptures!

GO and IMPLEMENT

- There are many "Déjà Vu" parallels between Bible characters even across the Testaments. Look for the similarities between Elijah and Jesus (like the fact that both do not eat for forty days in the wilderness) and then also look for even more numerous connections between Elisha and Jesus (like both raise a widow's son from the dead and both start their ministries at the Jordan River).

- Paul's life mirrors Jesus' life in many ways. Look for all the parallel situations at the end of Paul's life with the last days of Jesus in Luke's writings (Luke and Acts). Ponder what Luke is trying to communicate by having readers experience a "Déjà Vu" encounter between those two influential characters. For instance, both Jesus and Paul break bread and give thanks before a harrowing experience (Luke 24:30; Acts 27:35) and both are tried four times and declared innocent three times.

FOR FURTHER STUDY

Block, Daniel I. "Echo Narrative Technique in Hebrew Literature: A Study in Judges 19." *Westminster Theological Journal* 52, no. 2 (1990): 325–41.

Sailhamer, John. *Introduction to Old Testament Theology: A Canonical Approach.* Grand Rapids: Zondervan, 1995. (Appendix C)

Schnittjer, Gary E. *The Torah Story: An Apprenticeship on the Pentateuch.* Grand Rapids: Zondervan, 2006. (Chapter 1)

Test Case:
Book of Daniel

Let's look at the book of Daniel and apply these techniques to see what we can glean by implementing what has been taught in this book.

FIRST IMPRESSIONS

PHYSICAL DESCRIPTOR: Daniel 1:4 identifies the traits that Nebuchadnezzar looks for in foreign advisers such as Daniel. They must be "youths without blemish, of good appearance and skillful in all wisdom, endowed with knowledge, understanding learning, and competent to stand in the king's palace." Not only is this a good overall portrait of Daniel, but it stresses that he is "without blemish." Sometimes physical descriptors not only detail a character's outward appearance but imply spiritual traits as well.

For instance, in Genesis 27:1, Isaac is described as blind near the end of his life. The rest of the chapter reveals his other senses are also diminished, and because he appears to be close to death, he desires to bless his firstborn (even though he goes on to live for more than twenty years!). That chapter portrays Isaac more sensually (all five senses are mentioned) than spiritually, so the author foregrounds his diminished physical senses in tandem with his lack of spiritual awareness.

In this case, Daniel is "without blemish," which could imply that he not only has no physical imperfections but also is "without blemish" spiritually and morally. Sure enough, throughout the book, Daniel has no detectable flaws. In Daniel 1:4 he is also described as being of "good appearance." In many biblical passages, whenever a person is described as being physically attractive, readers can expect difficulty to arise due to that beauty (e.g., Sarah in Genesis 12:11, Rachel in Genesis 29:17, Tamar in 2 Samuel 13:1, Bathsheba in 2 Samuel 11:2, Vashti in Esther 1:10–11, Joseph in Genesis 39:6, Saul in 1 Samuel 9:2, David in 1 Samuel 16:18, Absalom in 2 Samuel 14:25). This makes Daniel's life stand out all the more in that his unblemished physical features are matched by his unblemished character and faithfulness to the Lord throughout his entire life.

FIRST ACTIONS: The first thing we see Daniel doing as we read the book is that he "resolved that he would not defile himself with the king's food, or with the wine that he drank" (Dan. 1:8). These actions portray Daniel as a man of conviction, which is another trait seen throughout the book, such as when he continues to pray toward Jerusalem even when commanded not to (Dan. 6:10).

FIRST WORDS: The first words that Daniel utters in the book are "test your servants for ten days; let us be given vegetables to eat and water to drink" (Dan. 1:12). His own opening words once again convey a willingness to stand on his principles from God's law and be tested on those convictions. Throughout the book, Daniel is repeatedly "tested" for his faith, and these opening words prepare the reader for multiple trials Daniel will undergo.

This "First Impressions" technique helps to provide a thumbnail portrait of Daniel as a man without blemish, with solid convictions, and with a willingness to put his commitment to God and His Word to the test.

READ THE LABELS

As readers we know that the main character in the book is none other than Daniel. However, the chief of the eunuchs assigned him a Babylonian name: "Belteshazzar" (1:7). It is helpful to track when the main character is referred to as "Daniel" and when he is referred to as "Belteshazzar." Daniel's identity as a Hebrew is contrasted with his Babylonian name. As one tracks those labels, the reader can see that the king (or his officials) are the only ones to ever use the Belteshazzar name in his presence. Somehow, Daniel is still able to maintain his Hebrew identity even in the midst of the Babylonian court. Daniel's own life demonstrates that it doesn't matter what others think of you, or even how they label you (e.g., Bible-thumper), and that it is entirely possible with God's grace and wisdom to maintain your spiritual identity in pagan environments.

Daniel 3:3 lists the "labels" of all the court officials:

Then the satraps, the prefects, and the governors, the coun-
selors, the treasurers, the justices, the magistrates, and all the
officials of the provinces gathered for the dedication of the
image that King Nebuchadnezzar had set up. And they stood
before the image that Nebuchadnezzar had set up.

The cumulative effect of taking the time to list every type
of imaginable official not only demonstrates the breadth of
the Babylonian bureaucracy but also elevates the tension that
Shadrach, Meshach, and Abednego will experience in the face of
such combined political peer pressure.

In Daniel 3, Shadrach, Meshach, and Abednego are always
called by those names and never mentioned by other terms such
as "Daniel's friends," "they," or their Hebrew names. Daniel was
able to keep his Hebrew identity intact even though he was assigned the pagan name of Belteshazzar (1:6), and Shadrach,
Meshach, and Abednego were as well, even though their given
Hebrew names were Hananiah, Mishael, and Azariah (Dan. 1:6).
They are not labeled as Daniel's "friends" here (even though they
are) because the author wants readers to see they are not riding
on the coattails of Daniel's prestige and respect (in fact, Daniel is
not mentioned by name or referenced anywhere in this chapter!)
but are able to withstand the test with God's help (Dan. 3:17).

Jerusalem has several labels in the book: "your city," "your
holy hill" (9:16), "city that bears your name" (9:18), "holy city"
(9:24). These various titles should help the reader recall the dedication of the temple in Jerusalem (1 Kings 8). In Daniel 6:10, it

is stated that Daniel prayed in the direction of Jerusalem (three times a day in fact!) in direct obedience of 1 Kings 8:46–53.

STEP UP TO THE MIC

In Daniel 1:12–13, we read Daniel's first recorded words:

> "Test your servants for ten days; let us be given vegetables to eat and water to drink. Then let our appearance and the appearance of the youths who eat the king's food be observed by you, and deal with your servants according to what you see."

Daniel's own words reveal that he was willing to be put to the test to demonstrate faithfulness to the Lord by not defiling himself with the king's food, and he did so in a wise, nonconfrontational way. The author of Daniel is subtly promoting Daniel's character and actions as a good role model for readers to emulate.

Daniel 1:10 records the speech of the Babylonian commander of the officials who Daniel approached to be relieved of eating the king's food.

> "I fear my lord the king, who assigned your food and your drink; for why should he see that you were in worse condition than the youths who are of your own age? So you would endanger my head with the king."

Reporting the commander's exact words serves not only to reveal the fear that all court appointees felt in the Babylonian palace but also raises the tension level for the reader by hearing a firsthand response.

Daniel 2:20–23 lets readers hear David's own verbal reply in response to God revealing to him the king's dream.

"Blessed be the name of God forever and ever, to whom belong wisdom and might. He changes times and seasons; he removes kings and sets up kings; he gives wisdom to the wise and knowledge to those who have understanding; he reveals deep and hidden things; he knows what is in the darkness, and the light dwells with him. To you, O God of my fathers, I give thanks and praise, for you have given me wisdom and might, and have now made known to me what we asked of you, for you have made known to us the king's matter."

Notice how Daniel's own words are a succinct summary of the entire book! As readers "hear" his voice, they should be able to check off all the other passages in Daniel that illustrate specific points made in his testimony of praise. By indirect implication it also is encouraging readers that they too should praise God when He reveals wisdom to His servants.

Astute readers will also be able to track the interplay between narrated action and direct speeches from one of the characters. These speeches not only characterize the one speaking, but they often foreground themes that the author is stressing.

Another example of "Step Up to the Mic" is found in Daniel 6. Most of this chapter is in the hand of the narrator, who chronicles the account of Daniel in the lions' den. Throughout this chapter there are short direct speeches by Daniel, Darius, and the band of jealous court officials, all of which help to paint a character portrait of the ones speaking. However, there is one longer "Step Up to the Mic" moment in 6:25–27, which reads:

Then King Darius wrote to all the peoples, nations, and languages that dwell in all the earth: "Peace be multiplied to you. I make a decree, that in all my royal dominion people are to tremble and fear before the God of Daniel, for he is the living God, enduring forever; his kingdom shall never be destroyed, and his dominion shall be to the end. He delivers and rescues; he works signs and wonders in heaven and on earth, he who has saved Daniel from the power of the lions."

Notice how Darius' own words voice what might be another overarching theme of the entire book. Earlier we heard major themes of the book from the lips of Daniel (2:20–23), but now we hear another overarching theme of the book by a pagan outsider! Narrators often yield up the microphone to allow a character within the book to voice a prominent theme, and the book of Daniel is no exception.

LAUNCHING PAD

The content of Daniel 1 does a great job in setting up the reader for key themes highlighted in the book. The "wisdom" of Daniel is introduced (1:4, 17), which will play a prominent role throughout the book. The fact that Daniel had "understanding in all visions and dreams" (1:17) preps the reader for the multiple times that Daniel will utilize that skill throughout the book. The fact that Daniel encourages the chief of the eunuchs to "test" Daniel and his friends (1:12) sets up readers for other such tests that they will undergo in the book (Dan. 2; Dan. 3; Dan. 6).

BEAUTIFUL BOOKENDS

Several "Bookends" or inclusios are present in the book of Daniel.

The opening chapter of Daniel contains the phrase "in the third year" as well as the names "King Cyrus" and "Belteshazzar" (Dan. 1:1, 7, 21). Those components are mirrored in Daniel 10:1: "In the third year of Cyrus king of Persia a word was revealed to Daniel, who was named Belteshazzar." These repeated elements tie the beginning of the book with the start of the last narrative, which shows structural cohesion but also highlights Daniel's remarkable testimony as he is able to maintain covenant loyalty to the God of Israel in the midst of the Babylonian and Persian Empires. Daniel demonstrates that it is possible to maintain spiritual convictions in the face of the surrounding dominant pagan forces even when assigned a pagan name like Belteshazzar!

Daniel is described in 1:4 as being one "skillful in all *wisdom*," and in 1:17 as one to whom God gave "skill in all literature and *wisdom*," and in the last chapter, the text states that, regarding what has been communicated in the book, "none of the wicked shall understand, but those who are *wise* shall understand" (12:10b). Daniel embodies the "wisdom" trait that readers will need in order to understand and apply the contents of this book.

Daniel's diet also forms a bookend within the book. His refusal to eat the king's food but only vegetables for ten days (Dan. 1:5–16) is mirrored at the end of the book in Daniel 10:3: "I ate no delicacies, no meat or wine entered my mouth, nor did I anoint myself at all, for the full three weeks." Daniel's level of commitment throughout the book extends even to what he eats and drinks. Perhaps Paul was thinking about Daniel when he wrote 1 Corinthians 10:31: "So, whether you eat or drink, or whatever you do, do all to the glory of God."

OBJECT LESSONS

There does not appear to be a clear example of an "object lesson" in the book, but there is the symbolic use of animals to represent certain nations. The bear (7:5) and the ram (8:2–4) are almost universally thought to represent the later Medo-Persian Empire, and the goat (8:5–11) signifies the nation of Greece. Of course, there is also the use of lions in the book (Dan. 6), which are often depicted in Babylonian art, such as the striding lions from the Ishtar Gate. The fact that Daniel is victorious over animals often associated with ancient Near Eastern royalty shows the supremacy of the God of Israel over the pagan gods.

There is a clear association of "food" with Daniel to show how even his diet demonstrates his level of commitment to God and His laws (Dan. 1:12–19; 10:3). Daniel's faithfulness to the God of Israel is clearly demonstrated in something as commonplace as what he eats or doesn't eat, which is a reminder to us as readers about the level to which we can live out our walk before a watching pagan world.

POETIC DIAMONDS

"Poetic Diamonds" often overlap with "Step Up to the Mic," since direct speeches often have a poetic quality to them. In English

Bible translations, this can often be seen by formatting such as line indents or italic font to indicate poetic material. Daniel 2:20–23 and 6:26–27, which were also examples of "Step Up to the Mic," are examples of "Poetic Diamonds" that appear in Daniel.

Another example of this technique is in Daniel 4:3 when Nebuchadnezzar declares the following using synonymous parallelism (where the second line restates the first line in poetic fashion):

How great are his signs,
    how mighty his wonders!
His kingdom is an everlasting kingdom,
    and his dominion endures from generation to generation.

This "poetic diamond" is a succinct thematic and theological summary of what the surrounding text of Daniel 4 is stating in narrative form. The embedded poem works in tandem with the broader context to make that point emphatically clear. Identifying this technique will allow readers to understand the text's main takeaway, which is to extol God for the powerful way He works because His rule is eternal!

LOCATION, LOCATION, LOCATION

While Daniel is not full of geographical notations like other books, there are enough locations for the reader to pause and ponder their significance. Right away in Daniel 1:1–2 we learn about Babylon besieging Jerusalem, and the vessels of the temple were taken eastward to "Shinar." This draws the reader's attention to the Tower of Babel incident (see Gen. 11:1–11), which is another account surrounded by rebellion and eastward movement.

Mountains are mentioned five times within the book and tap into the notion of those locations as sacred space (e.g., Mount Sinai, Sermon on the Mount, Mount of Transfiguration). Daniel is by the banks of the river Tigris (10:4), where he receives a vision. Ezekiel, another prophet in Babylon, also receives a vision by a river (Ezek. 1). In this case, it is the Chebar river. Therefore, rivers seem to be ideal locations for God to reveal His plans to prophets due to the abundance of water for cleansing and for purification rituals (e.g., Moses at the Nile, Naaman instructed by the prophet Elisha to dip in the Jordan in 2 Kings 5:11, John the Baptist at the Jordan).

CLOCK MANAGEMENT

Daniel 9 shows an example of "Clock Management" when it slows down the pace to focus on Daniel's lengthy prayer. This allows the reader to clearly see Daniel's heart and commitment, which are traits that the biblical author wishes to see in the lives of the readers of this book.

OUT OF ORDER

The book of Daniel does not follow a strict chronology, and the wise reader will pick up on content that is not given in straightforward linear progression. For instance, Daniel 6 and 9 take place in the reign of Darius, a Persian king. But Daniel 5, 7, and 8 take place during the reign of Belshazzar, a Babylonian ruler. As a result, there is not chronological continuity as one reads this book. In this case, the chronological displacement is done for thematic and structural purposes, such as separating the narrative accounts (Dan. 1–6) from the vision accounts (Dan. 7–12).

YOU CAN SAY THAT AGAIN!

In Daniel 3 there is a lot of repetition for rhetorical effect:

- the various offices of court officials (3x—3:2, 3, 27)
- the names of the musical instruments (4x—3:5, 7, 10, 15)
- the image that Nebuchadnezzar "set up" (7x—3:1, 2, 3, 5, 7, 12, 14)
- "fiery furnace" (8x—3:6, 11, 15, 17, 20, 21, 23, 26)
- "Shadrach, Meshach, and Abednego" (13x—3:12, 13, 14, 16, 19, 20, 22, 23, 26[2x], 28, 29, 30)

The concentrated number of repetitions in this chapter were clearly intended by the author of the book of Daniel. The challenge for the reader is to not only recognize their presence but also slow down and ponder why the author would purposely include repetition. Since the author does not explain the rationale behind the repetition, readers will have to use some degree of sanctified imagination to ascertain their presence and function. We should exhibit caution and tentativeness rather than overconfidence in our conclusions about the author's unstated intentions. In many cases repeated words reveal a key theme or concept that the author wishes to foreground, which does not seem to be the case here with the frequent repetitions in this chapter that do not seem to surface a theological theme.

For example, why are the musical instruments repeated ad nauseam? The simplest explanation is that instead of the repetition being thematic, it is present to satirically portray the Babylonian Empire. In comedic fashion, the reader can sense the almost laughable scenario playing out over and over and over again while the narrator mocks those in charge who are orchestrating (no pun intended) this supposedly festive occasion!

X MARKS THE SPOT

Daniel is a book full of chiastic structures of all sizes: on the paragraph level, the chapter level, and even larger sections. Daniel 2–7 is an example of a broad chiasm:

Chapter 2: Vision of four great future kingdoms, climaxing with God's eternal kingdom

Chapter 3: God delivers His servants from death (fiery furnace)

Chapter 4: God is sovereign and humbles kings at will (Nebuchadnezzar)

Chapter 5: God is sovereign and humbles kings at will (Belshazzar)

Chapter 6: God delivers His servants from death (lions)

Chapter 7: Vision of four great future kingdoms, climaxing with God's eternal kingdom

The center of this chiasm focuses on the ability of the sovereign God of Israel to depose powerful, self-centered earthly monarchs. For the original readers, this should have been a powerful motivator to remain faithful to God and to keep His law even in the face of persecution and loss of self-governance.

For more examples of this technique used in the book of Daniel, check out chapter 26 of David Dorsey's *The Literary Structure of the Old Testament*.

HEADS UP

There is a bit of a "Heads Up" alert in that Daniel in 1:21 is said to continue to serve "until the first year of Cyrus the king." This signals to the reader ahead of time that despite all the tests and challenges that will come at Daniel by both Babylonian and Persian leadership, he will persevere and live a long life. Daniel's faithfulness to the Lord and to the law of Moses seen in chapter 1 will result in a long, prosperous life (Josh. 1:7–8).

In terms of foreshadowing within the book, the fact that the king found Daniel and his three friends "ten times better than all the magicians and enchanters that were in all his kingdom" (1:20) signals to the reader that hereafter, throughout the book, there will be plenty of opportunities for Daniel to display his superior wisdom and insight regarding the future.

DÉJÀ VU

There is a clear "Déjà Vu" example between Daniel and Joseph as the following chart demonstrates.

SIMILARITIES BETWEEN JOSEPH AND DANIEL		
Similarity	Joseph	Daniel
Taken out of their land as slaves	"Meanwhile the Midianites had sold him in Egypt to Potiphar, an officer of Pharaoh, the captain of the guard" (37:36).	"to bring some of the people of Israel" (1:3)
Separated from family as a teen	"Come, let us sell him to the Ishmaelites, and let not our hand be upon him, for he is our brother, our own flesh." And his brothers listened to him. Then Midianite traders passed by. And they drew Joseph up and lifted him out of the pit, and sold him to the Ishmaelites for twenty shekels of silver. They took Joseph to Egypt" (37:27–28).	"both of the royal family and of the nobility, youths without blemish" (1:3–4)
Served in a foreign court under Gentile rulers	"You shall be over my house, and all my people shall order themselves as you command. Only as regards the throne will I be greater than you" (41:40).	"competent to stand in the king's palace" (1:4)
Was assigned a new name	Zaphenath-paneah (41:45)	Belteshazzar (1:7)
Interpreted dreams	Interpreted the dreams of the cupbearer and baker and Pharaoh (Gen. 40; 41)	Interpreted two different dreams of Nebuchadnezzar (Dan. 2; 4)
Described as "wise"	"Then Pharaoh said to Joseph, 'Since God has shown you all this, there is none so discerning and wise as you are'" (41:39).	"And in every matter of wisdom and understanding about which the king inquired of them, he found them ten times better than all the magicians and enchanters that were in all his kingdom" (1:20).

Served in the most powerful nation at the time	"Joseph was thirty years old when he entered the service of Pharaoh king of Egypt" (41:46).	"And the king spoke with them, and among all of them none was found like Daniel, Hananiah, Mishael, and Azariah. Therefore they stood before the king [Nebuchadnezzar]" (1:19).
Rose to great prominence	"And Pharaoh said to Joseph, 'See, I have set you over all the land of Egypt'" (41:41).	"Then the king gave Daniel high honors and many great gifts, and made him ruler over the whole province of Babylon and chief prefect over all the wise men of Babylon" (2:48).
Underwent a test and suffering	Potiphar's wife lied and he was falsely imprisoned for two years (Gen. 39).	Daniel and the lion's den (Dan. 6).
Played a role in preserving their people	"'As for you, you meant evil against me, but God meant it for good, to bring it about that many people should be kept alive, as they are today. So do not fear; I will provide for you and your little ones.' Thus he comforted them and spoke kindly to them" (50:20–21).	"So the decree went out, and the wise men were about to be killed; and they sought Daniel and his companions, to kill them" (2:13). "Daniel made a request of the king, and he appointed Shadrach, Meshach, and Abednego over the affairs of the province of Babylon" (2:49).
Was the victim of a jealous plot	Potiphar's wife sought to seduce him and then lied about him (Gen. 39).	"Then the high officials and the satraps sought to find a ground for complaint against Daniel with regard to the kingdom, but they could find no ground for complaint or any fault, because he was faithful, and no error or fault was found in him" (6:4).
Both cast into a place of confinement	"And Joseph's master took him and put him into the prison, the place where the king's prisoners were confined, and he was there in prison" (39:20).	"Then the king commanded, and Daniel was brought and cast into the den of lions" (6:16).

Gold chain given as honor	"Then Pharaoh took his signet ring from his hand and put it on Joseph's hand, and clothed him in garments of fine linen and put a gold chain about his neck" (41:42).	"Then Belshazzar gave the command, and Daniel was clothed with purple, a chain of gold was put around his neck, and a proclamation was made about him, that he should be the third ruler in the kingdom" (5:29).

There are so many linkages for these two wise Hebrews who rose to prominence in a foreign court. It is easy to make comparisons because there are so many similarities between them that it cannot be chalked up to mere coincidence. It provides a "Déjà Vu" experience for readers who are expected to think back to Joseph's experiences when they read the book of Daniel.

One clear takeaway for readers is to remember that God can infiltrate His messengers into even the highest circles of pagan power as evidence of His superiority! It may look like those opposed to God have all the power, but God can plant His servants to do His bidding anywhere in the world. Readers can take examples like this and look for contrasts. Daniel always maintained his Hebrew identity, whereas Joseph was thoroughly Egyptianized (even his own brothers could not recognize him). As good as Joseph was, Daniel seems to take it even further by his total dedication to God and obedience to His Word.

PRACTICAL APPLICATIONS AND TAKEAWAYS

The book of Daniel is a great showcase for the fresh ways you can enjoy the Bible described in this book. Not only do these techniques reveal the stunning literary artistry of the Scriptures, but they also reveal key themes within the book and practical truths that can be applied to your life today.

Let's review just two of the key theological principles from Daniel that surfaced as a result of utilizing "X Marks the Spot":

1) God is sovereign over rulers and kingdoms.
2) God rewards obedience to those faithful to Him and humbles those who are proud.

You may feel overwhelmed by the fact that you, as an individual, are seemingly powerless against all the spiritual, moral, and national strongholds that control the levers of power. Be encouraged after your fresh reading of Daniel and learning from these techniques—God is still in control over individual leaders, nations, and political strongholds! That doesn't necessarily mean that we as believers will not be affected by these powerful forces and entities but that God, in His timetable, will accomplish His plans and purposes. He will reward and use humble obedient servants as change agents and humiliate those who display arrogance.

You will discover that looking for specific ways to apply the Bible will be much easier to do once you begin regularly utilizing the techniques discussed in this book. You will now have a tuned ear and clear eye to hear and see more of how the biblical authors designed the content of these texts and what they wished to foreground. These techniques equip you with fresh ways to enjoy your Bible and also reveal discernible action points based on what the biblical author was intending to communicate. As a result, the living Word can truly be displayed in your day-to-day walk with the Lord.

FOR FURTHER STUDY

Dorsey, David A. *The Literary Structure of the Old Testament.* Grand Rapids: Baker, 1999. (Chapter 26)

Hamilton, James M. *With the Clouds of Heaven: The Book of Daniel in Biblical Theology.* Downers Grove, IL: InterVarsity Press, 2014.

Zone of Turbulence

SUMMARY: This is not a new technique but rather a combination of multiple techniques described in this book, occurring in close proximity to each other in a single passage. This creates a "Zone of Turbulence"[28] and indicates a peak or point of prominence in the text. Biblical authors can create a disruption to the normal prototypical writing pattern readers have been experiencing or have come to expect, which consequently causes readers to be more sensitive to what they are reading. This turbulence has a positive impact for readers because it signals texts that have more prominence in terms of the author's thematic agenda.

PREVALENCE: By their very nature, literary zones of turbulence are not commonplace because not all texts can be a discourse peak, and they would lose their rhetorical force if all passages exhibited this phenomenon.

INSTRUCTION: Literary zones of turbulence often go hand in hand with texts that readers already intuitively sense have prominence (e.g., Gen. 22; 1 Sam. 17). When the biblical author piles up rhetorical elements with a higher frequency in these texts, they have more literary magnetism that draws the reader's attention disproportionately as compared to surrounding chapters. A good place to begin is to identify passages that people tend to favor naturally and then investigate those texts for the frequency of devices described in this book. If multiple literary features are present that are not as prevalent in the surrounding passages, chances are high that you have evidence for a literary "Zone of Turbulence."

VALUE/PAYOFF: Literary zones of turbulence are profitable in that they indicate a thematic peak or a place of prominence or climax in the overall flow of the biblical book, which helps readers ascertain key notions that the author is seeking to highlight.

CHALLENGES: Identifying literary zones of turbulence may not be easy at first, but it will get easier once readers become familiarized with the literary devices at a biblical author's disposal.

EXAMPLES FROM NONBIBLICAL WORKS:
The Wizard of Oz (1939): After the tornado has carried her house to a new place, Dorothy exclaims: "Toto, I have a feeling we're not in Kansas anymore." There is a transition of a new setting (clearly evidenced by the switch from black and white

to color in stunning contrast), tension with the house falling on the Wicked Witch of the East, character development revealing Dorothy's naivete, and of course the iconic line about Kansas. These elements all converge in high density to demonstrate that this is a peak moment in the film thematically.

The Empire Strikes Back (1980): A good example of a "Zone of Turbulence" in this film is the scene where Darth Vader, at the end of a lightsaber duel with Luke Skywalker, says "I am your father." The scene is stacked with multiple visual and audio storytelling techniques: the precarious backdrop, the heat of intense struggle in battle, the heightened emotions, a significant reveal in a direct speech, and the earlier foreshadowing in the film where Luke has a vision of himself beheading Darth Vader with a lightsaber (only to realize that the head in the shadowy helmet is his own) all are embedded in this scene. This concentration of these elements demonstrate that this is a prominent scene in the film.

If you fly on airplanes regularly, you will inevitably encounter turbulence. The plane will be at a smooth cruising altitude when it suddenly encounters some rough air and begins to shake. The captain announces on the intercom that passengers should return to their seats and buckle their seat belts until the "fasten seat belt" indicator turns off. During those times, passengers tend to be a little more conscious of their surroundings and have a heightened sense of alertness that they normally don't have when flying without turbulence.

This is similar to how we can experience reading the Bible. We can experience smooth sailing for quite some time but then encounter a text that, through some external or internal elements, heightens our awareness of the current context. While turbulence is often viewed negatively while flying, turbulence while reading is actually a good thing because it signals a peak or place of prominence due to its importance.

"ZONE OF TURBULENCE" IN GENESIS 22

Genesis 22 might be the most quintessential example of a literary "Zone of Turbulence." It is the pinnacle of Old Testament narratives. It is a text that drips with emotion and drama, yet very few words from the semantic domain of emotions are utilized except for one mention of "love" in 22:2 (which makes that sole occurrence stand out even more!).

LOCATION, LOCATION, LOCATION: The main event takes place on a mountain (22:2, 14), which is a prominent geographical setting used in other biblical accounts (Mount Sinai, Mount Carmel, Mount of Transfiguration, etc.).

READ THE LABELS: A variety of terms are used to reference deity or divine figures: God (Elohim) (vv. 1, 3, 8, 9, 12); LORD (vv. 14[2x], 16); angel of the LORD (vv. 11, 15).

STEP UP TO THE MIC: This passage contains a high degree of back-and-forth dialogue of direct speeches as compared to other

Abraham passages. It also includes the speech that provides the thematic summary statement of the account: "God will provide for himself the lamb for a burnt offering, my son" (Gen. 22:8).

X MARKS THE SPOT: There is a clear chiastic structure embedded in this chapter, which pivots around 22:8.

A. your son, your only son (v. 2)
   B. the place his God had mentioned to him (v. 3)
      C. the two of them went along together (v. 6)
         D. my son (v. 7)
            E. God will provide for Himself the lamb for the
               burnt offering (v. 8)
         D'. my son (v. 8)
      C'. the two of them went along together (v. 8)
   B'. the place his God had mentioned to him (v. 9)
A'. your son, your only son (v. 12)

OBJECT LESSONS: At least two objects here in this passage could be construed as "Object Lessons." One is an altar, which is associated with texts in Genesis involving Abraham: Shechem (12:6–7), Bethel (12:8–9), Hebron (13:14–18), and here at Moriah (22:9). According to author Benjamin Noonan, the altars in Genesis are built at strategic sites in Canaan in passages that reference the inhabitants who serve as obstacles to the land promise.[29] Another object lesson is trees/wood. Isaac carries the wood that his father Abraham personally cut (22:2, 6–7). Throughout Abraham's life, there are multiple references to trees. (See chapter 6 on "Object Lessons" for more details.)

POETIC DIAMONDS: The speech by the angel of the Lord in 22:16–18 is set in lyrical form, reiterating and strengthening the original promise given to Abram in Genesis 12: "By myself I have sworn, declares the LORD, because you have done this and have not withheld your son, your only son, I will surely bless you, and I will surely multiply your offspring as the stars of heaven and as the sand that is on the seashore. And your offspring shall possess the gate of his enemies, and in your offspring shall all the nations of the earth be blessed, because you have obeyed my voice." This lyrical statement demonstrates Abraham's faith and obedience, beautifully tying in God's original promise to Abram back in Genesis 12.

OUT OF ORDER: The author interrupts the narrative timeline of the actual chronological order of events in the chapter to interject a later period when the text was actually written down. This mention refers to a time long after Abraham experienced the events of this chapter. In 22:14 we read:

> So Abraham called the name of that place, "The LORD will provide"; *as it is said to this day*, "On the mount of the LORD it shall be provided."

The author wants readers to be aware that, at the time of writing, the place still has the name "The LORD will provide." This place name confirms the main thematic goal of this text, and its significance is stated to linger long beyond when the original event took place.

A subtle example of "Out of Order" is found in 22:3: "So Abraham rose early in the morning, *saddled his donkey*, and took two of his young men with him, and his son Isaac. And he cut the wood for the burnt offering and arose and went to the place of which God had told him." The expected order of Abraham's actions that morning would be to saddle his donkey *after* cutting the wood, not before, since you want the pack animal to be as comfortable as possible before undertaking a long journey.

The fact that Abraham did things out of order from the expected way may give us a little window into the agonizing frame of mind Abraham was in that morning. He is wanting to be obedient to God's command, so he gets up early (or perhaps he couldn't sleep well after hearing the command the day before!). His brain is not functionally logically, so he keeps himself busy (even though he has many trained servants to do that kind of work) with making preparations for the journey to help keep his mind off things, but not in the order one normally follows in preparing for a trip.

CLOCK MANAGEMENT: There is a flurry of actions that Abraham accomplishes in 22:3 (i.e., he rose, he saddled, he took, he cut, he arose, he went). This has the effect of speeding up the pace, but then the dialogues of 22:5–8 slow down that pace to a crawl. The fast pace of 22:3 appears to be included to demonstrate that Abraham is "keeping himself busy" to avoid thinking too much about the agony of what God has just asked him to do. The slowing down of the pace so that we hear the exact words of Abraham and Isaac as they converse with other helps the reader to ponder the importance of what was communicated in this tense moment. In this section we "hear" Abraham reveal a key theme of the passage in 22:8—that the Lord is a God who provides in times of need.

YOU CAN SAY THAT AGAIN!: This passage contains repetition of key words and phrases:

- son (22:2[2x], 3, 6, 7, 10, 12[2x])
- so they went both of them together (22:6, 8)
- Abraham raised his eyes (22:4, 13)
- the place of which God told him (22:3, 9)

All these repeated words and phrases foreground key themes and thrusts embedded in the passage, such as the importance of the seed line, obedience, and "seeing" God's provision (hence the name of the place "the LORD will see/provide").

As we can see, the author loaded up this passage with multiple literary devices. The frequency and density of these elements combine to make sure that the reader experiences and views this as a key prominent peak text in the Abraham narrative. This literary "Zone of Turbulence" foregrounds a key pivotal passage in Genesis. Now the reader has objective evidence to know why they naturally gravitated to the importance of this text to begin with, due to the high density of indicators of literary prominence.

Like many people, I enjoy shooting off fireworks with my family, especially with my grandchildren present. To see the look of wonder and amazement on their faces is a joy to behold as they experience what pyrotechnics can do. But those backyard productions pale in comparison to the extravaganzas that local municipalities put on celebrating the Fourth of July. Even then, it is the grand finale at those events that elicit the most oohs and aahs.

That is how we experience the Scriptures. There is always

amazement whenever we open God's Word, but on occasion, some passages just seem to overwhelm us with their beauty and impact. As we have learned in this chapter, those peak texts are designed by the biblical authors for such an impact because they stack literary techniques on top of each other, much like the burst of multiple shells at the conclusion of a Fourth of July fireworks display.

Just as those events are put on to celebrate key themes of the American experience, such as freedom and self-determination, so these literary "Zone of Turbulence" texts foreground foundational spiritual themes like the necessity of faith and obedience and the Lord's ability to constantly provide all we need as we trust Him. Those truths are to be celebrated and lived out in our present-day walk as well!

GO and IMPLEMENT

GENESIS 1 is a literary "Zone of Turbulence." Try to identify all the literary features and techniques that Moses inserted into this chapter and how they foreground key biblical themes and foreshadow later events in the Pentateuch.

1 SAMUEL 17 is another chapter with multiple literary devices. Search for as many devices as you can and summarize how they could be seen as advancing the thematic purposes of 1 and 2 Samuel.

Bonus Reading Guidelines

In addition to the specific techniques talked about in this book on how to enjoy your Bible, here are some general guidelines on how to maximize your reading of God's Word.

Read repeatedly

The Bible assumes that one is going to read it over and over again. In fact, there are some passages that share events that happen later with the assumption that subsequent readings will give more context to the earlier story when we get around to rereading the passage. For instance, Genesis 13:10 refers to the destruction of Sodom and Gomorrah before the event is described in Genesis 19 because it presupposes that a reader will make a deeper connection on the second (and subsequent) reading. In hermeneutics, this process of repeated readings is called the "hermeneutical spiral,"[30] whereby the process of "interpretation entails a 'spiral'

from text to context, from its original meaning to its contextu-
alization or significance for the church today."[31] It is not a circle
where one just simply goes around and around, but rather, upon
each subsequent reading, the reader spirals closer and closer to
the text's intended meaning. With each reading, we can engage it
on a different level because of previous exposure to the material.

Read whole books in one sitting

Many people who read the Bible only do so in small chunks.
They may be following a daily devotional or even an organized
Bible reading plan, and both of those methods have their place,
but there is nothing more valuable than reading an entire book of
the Bible in one sitting, because then you are more likely to pick
up on themes that are much harder to detect when only reading
a paragraph or a chapter at a time. In the amount of time that one
can sit and watch a movie (generally two to three hours) one can
actually start and complete the reading of a number of individual
books of the Bible. There are certainly large books that will take
longer to read, but even the longest book of the Bible (Jeremiah)
can typically be done in under eight hours. Therefore it is possible, if one takes the time and effort to commit to it. The goal of
this reading is not to focus on minute details of the text but to let
large passages of the text enter your mind to capture the flow of
events and see things from the big picture.

Read in multiple versions

Reading the Bible in different translations can prompt new
insights for the reader. It is good to read versions with different translation philosophies. Some Bibles are more formal and

follow the underlying original language more closely (like the New American Standard Bible). Others are more functional and try to capture the sense of the original text in readable English (like the New International Version).

Both translation philosophies have their strengths and weaknesses. For instance, as was mentioned earlier, repetition is harder to see in functional versions since they tend to vary translating the underlying original language words with different English words based on modern stylistics. Functional versions do a better job of unpacking the meaning of idioms and metaphors but are not conducive for deeper analytical study. English Bible readers have the luxury of benefiting from various translations available, so taking advantage of those versions can lead to great personal profit.

Listen orally

Before the advent of the printing press, most people's intake of God's Word was through the ear and not the eye. While it is beneficial to read the words of the text with your own eyes, there is much to be gained by also listening to it. Your ear may do a better job of picking up repeated words or clauses. Any oral reading of the Bible involves some degree of subjective interpretation depending on the tone, pitch, and voice. For instance, how one recites God's question to Adam after the fall in Genesis 3:9 ("Where are you?") is interpretive because it can be read with an angry tone or with a gentle, beckoning voice (or anywhere in between). Even with the subjective interpretations that come from such recitations, it can be a very profitable method of intake because it might stimulate new observations about the text.

Read "actively," not "passively"

Do not be a passive reader that just focuses on the facts and data (people, places, and events) presented in the text. Instead, have a healthy degree of internal dialogue with the author, contemplating why some details are inserted and others are left out. Ponder why accounts are next to others and if there might be a thread (theme) that the author is weaving into the overall flow of the text. We should certainly avoid having a critical spirit and approach the text with humility, recognizing that it is God's eternal Word, but we should also not be afraid to ask tough, engaging questions.

Read with expectation

Approach the biblical text with a trembling heart (Isa. 66:2), expecting that you will learn as you interact with God's revealed revelation. Even though the Bible can be approached like any other book and studied on purely an academic basis, it is a far better strategy as a believer to come to the written revealed Word of God with the stance that the Spirit of God zealously wants you to engage the text with your heart wide open to receive truth from its eternal pages. A popular saying goes like this: "two things last forever: people and the Word of God." Since God's Word is eternal and comes from an infinite God, we are more than likely to continue engaging it in eternity. So, it is best to come with an expectant heart and mind and allow it to continually shape and mold us.

Read without focusing on chapter breaks or verse divisions

Chapter breaks and verse divisions are helpful because they offer a clear road map for those who engage the Scriptures. This makes sure everyone is looking at the same passage, particularly in a sermon or group Bible study. However, what serves as an advantage for a community's interaction with the Word of God can sometimes be detrimental for individual Bible study, since those numbers and divisions can be a distraction or cause readers to miss the author's flow of thought.

Chapter divisions were introduced by Stephen Langton and have only been around since the thirteenth century, and Robert Estienne added verse numbers in the sixteenth century.[32] So both systems were developed long after the biblical authors composed the individual books. These numerical divisions make it more challenging for the reader to follow the author's thought process because they inject an arbitrary structure onto the content at times. Readers can miss certain connections simply because an ensuing chapter break is inserted.

One of the clearest examples of a chapter break that interrupts the natural flow is between Genesis 1 and 2. Genesis 2:1–3 actually fits better with the context of Genesis 1, so if there is a division break, it should occur after 2:3 and not where it is presently located.

Thankfully there are now several reader's versions of the Bible that have removed the chapter numbers and verse breaks that make such a reading an easier process (for instance, the *ESV Reader's Bible*).

Read first and then study deeper

Many Bible readers attempt to do a deep study of the Bible as soon as they begin to read the text. They immediately embark on in-depth analysis of individual words and cross-references. It will most likely be more profitable if you read the entire content of the text in repeated continuous readings before embarking on a detailed analysis of a smaller text. This way, you have more of the author's train of thought in mind so that when you come back around to do a more detailed analysis, you are less likely to pursue theological or thematic rabbit trails that may have nothing to do with what the author is intending for readers to ponder. Allow the author to shape what you pursue in a more thorough way rather than taking a disorganized approach that lacks focus.

Consider reading the biblical books using different arrangements of their ordering

Most readers today are guided in the way they read by the traditional order found in most Protestant Bibles. Many are surprised to learn that the ordering of the books by the apostle Paul in the New Testament are arranged, for the most part, in descending order based on length. That means that Romans and 1 and 2 Corinthians are the first books readers of the New Testament epistles encounter due to their length rather than by when they were composed. Galatians would most likely be the first epistle you would read if Paul's writings were arranged chronologically. So, if you want to see the theological progression of Paul's books based on the order in which he wrote them, you would have to read them in a different order than which they are currently placed.

Another example is Luke–Acts. The gospel of Luke and the book of Acts (both authored by Luke) are separated in our Bibles with the gospel of John in between them, but it is helpful to read them back-to-back to follow Luke's complete train of thought.

In the Old Testament, the book of Ruth is typically read after Judges because it depicts events that take place during the book of Judges (Ruth 1:1). Although, you have to wonder why the book was not simply included at the end of the book of Judges, since there seems to be a "Bethlehem trilogy"[33] of stories: the Levite from Bethlehem (Judg. 17–18), the concubine from Bethlehem (Judg. 19–21), and the book of Ruth, which takes place in Bethlehem. In each case, a man leaves Bethlehem under less-than-ideal circumstances.

In Hebrew Bibles, which follow a different ordering tradition called TaNaK—an acronym for Torah (the Law), Nevi'im (the Prophets), and Ketuvim (the Writings)—there is a different order of books, which can provide for meaningful observations. For instance, in some Hebrew Bibles the book of Ruth follows the book of Proverbs (in the "writings" section), which allows one to see the connection between the Proverbs 31 virtuous women (*ishit hayil*, v. 10) with a clear example of what that looks like in the person of Ruth, as Boaz uses that same phrase to refer to her (Ruth 3:11).

Familiarize yourself with key terminology

Part of Adam's job description in exercising dominion over creation was to name all the animals. Labeling (and naming) is helpful for categorizing and making sense of the world. The same is true in approaching our study of God's Word. The more vocabulary you have to describe what you are reading and observing in the text is just a part of exercising dominion. For instance, describing biblical characters as either being "round" or "flat" (using terms that E. M. Forster coined in his book *Aspects of the Novel*) can help to classify characters for deeper reflection. Round characters such as Abram, David, or Paul are complex and show development, and flat characters such as Lot's wife and Gehazi are two-dimensional with little variation in their actions and attitudes.

Every occupation has a unique set of terms that one must know and navigate if they are to demonstrate mastery of their discipline. For instance, carpenters should not only know that a certain tool is a hammer, but they need to know what kind of hammer (i.e., claw, ball-peen, sledge, etc.) so that they select the right one for the job. Since the Bible is a literary text, it is beneficial to know the names and definitions of literary devices and the functions they have in different genres.

Be comfortable with degrees of certainty and uncertainty

Readers often want straightforward answers to questions they have when they read the Bible. They seek a definitive black-and-white response to issues they are interested in. Sometimes readers have a clear understanding of what the text's main thrust is about; other times it appears as though the meaning has to be slowly coaxed out of its shell to reveal what the author is focusing on. Remember, sometimes the Bible contains directives that are easily discernible, such as Paul's direct command to Timothy in 2 Timothy 2:22: "So flee youthful passions and pursue righteousness, faith, love, and peace." Other times (especially in narrative texts), the author's intention as to why a passage is included in the Bible is more subtle.

When readers are more confident in their understanding

of the text's purpose, they can be more forthright in proclaiming the text's intention with a high degree of certainty. In other passages, there may be some hints as to what the biblical authors are driving at, but the degree of certainty is not as high. In those cases, it is critical that we be more tentative when communicating the text's purpose.

Live with the tension in the text

Sometimes Scriptures seem at odds with one another. In an effort to reduce such conflict, some feel compelled to soften that tension and "flatten" the seemingly contradictory statements to "help" the Bible out. The beauty of God's Word is that it speaks to a variety of circumstances, and while one passage may be pertinent in one setting, it may not be as helpful in another scenario. One example of this is Proverbs 26:4–5, which states:

> Answer not a fool according to his folly,
> lest you be like him yourself.
> Answer a fool according to his folly,
> lest he be wise in his own eyes.

Critics of the Bible often point to verses like these to prove that the Bible is full of contradictions and is therefore untrustworthy.

However, by living with the tension here, we find a powerful insight from the author. These two opposite injunctions are found side by side in the book of Proverbs, which is designed to instill wisdom in those who read it and heed it (Prov. 1:1–7).

In real-life situations, there are different types of "fools" that we encounter: ignorant fools who simply lack knowledge and need instruction, and stubborn fools who are unteachable no matter how much effort one puts forth to help them. For stubborn fools, Proverbs 26:4 basically tells us not to waste our time in addressing them, lest you become more like they are. On the other hand, when it comes to ignorant fools, there is benefit in seeking to coach them so they don't proceed down the path toward becoming an obstinate fool.

In other words, there are two different types of fools, and one needs "wisdom" (which is what Proverbs is seeking to foster) to know whether to address or avoid them altogether. Every parent and teacher needs to know whether their child or student needs a confidence-building motivational talk or a firm, corrective rebuke. Likewise, the Bible assumes that readers of the text will have enough situational awareness and spiritual sensitivity to know when to apply different passages of Scripture that, on the surface, seem at tension with each other. This requires that we pay close attention to the context.

Verbal priority

A good rule of thumb to observe while you are reading is to focus on verbs. Verbs are the main weight-bearing part of speech in any language, so more focus should be given to them as they are action-oriented. It is not that other parts of speech are not important. It is just that authors use verbs as the melody line of every text, and they must be attended to first if one wants to track along with the author. Verbs set the time frame of an action (past, present, and future). Verbs frame whether an action is a truth claim or whether it is a command.

So, what do you look for once you focus on the verbs in a text? Pay attention to the verbs that are used and see if there are any patterns embedded by their use. For instance, is there focus on verbs of motion (walking, running, going up, going down) or speech verbs (said, spoke, proclaimed)? Is there a cascade of action verbs to speed up the pace of a story or does it slow momentum down by injecting a direct speech quote by one of the characters within the story?

Foregrounding/Backgrounding

While every word in the text is inspired, it does not mean that every word is equally important in any given passage. Some words (especially verbs) are foregrounded by the author and carry more weight linguistically. For instance, finite verbs are typically more significant in determining the meaning of a passage than indefinite articles. Some parts of speech are simply there to set the stage so that the foregrounded material stands out more as you read. Once you hone your reading strategy, it should be easier to detect what the author is focusing on.

Think of the biblical text as a 3D topographical map. When one first looks at such a map, there are certain features that tend to stand out, such as major mountains or bodies of water. In addition, there are numerous small valleys and hills that fill out the frame dominated by the main topographical features. So it is with the biblical text. There are some features that are foregrounded and are core components of the passage as well as smaller details that are part of the discourse, but it would not be productive to focus on those details unless the main components lead you to do so.

Big picture versus detailed picture

Many Bible readers seek to make observations on every word in a passage. While that can lead to some valuable insights, it can also distract from following the author's main line of thought if the reader is focusing on a subpoint rather than a main point. Those detailed analytical skills are critical, but it is better to get the broader picture first and then, after isolating the main themes or ideas, drill down with more detailed analysis and focus on other details in the text. The goal is to get the lay of the land first before you begin pulling out a microscope to study details.

We need a general awareness of the forest before analyzing the leaves. Most Bible study methods start by giving Bible readers inductive skills that tend to focus on detailed analysis. The skills learned in this book should help to develop a reading strategy that discovers the big picture before diving into all the finer points. That way, there is a scaffold on which to hang any observations made during a more detailed analysis of the text.

Learn to pose better text-centered questions as you read

Many Bible readers are accustomed to raise questions as they read, which is a good technique to stay engaged. However, oftentimes questions posed are more curiosity questions that stem from the modern world and are not necessarily questions that the original readers would have pondered. A typical curiosity question is: "Where do dinosaurs fit in the Genesis 1 account?" Now that may be an interesting question from a modern reader's perspective, but it is not something that Moses intentionally set out to address when that text was originally written. Instead, we should first seek to understand what the text is aiming to address (i.e., humanity being made in the image of God and Sabbath as the pinnacle of the creation week).

Persevere!

Some texts provide clear insights and use obvious literary devices that stand out. Other texts are much more elusive and seemingly need to be coaxed a bit to divulge what they are about. Once you have learned some of the skills described in this book, you may have to attempt implementing multiple techniques before you start to yield productive insights. Some texts will utilize several of the techniques while others may use them sparingly. So, if one of these does not seem productive, move on to others and you may find one of those more revealing. Some texts require that they simmer and stew in your mind for a while rather than a quick microwave approach with instant results. Hang in there! God's Word is worth the effort and you will be rewarded over and over again with fresh discoveries.

Acknowledgments

I would like to thank Julius Wong Loi Sing, not only for his friendship but also for the multiple conversations we have had together over the years sharpening the concepts presented in this book. In addition, I am grateful to Rosie de Rosset for stimulating conversation over the years about how authors go about crafting literary masterpieces. I would also like to thank Ajit and Katie Christopher and my wife, Gayle, for their valuable suggestions on aspects of this book. In addition, I owe a deep debt of gratitude to Randall Payleitner and Connor Sterchi for their expert editorial skills in helping this book become a reality.

Notes

1. Howard Hendricks and William Hendricks, *Living by the Book: The Art and Science of Reading the Bible* (Chicago: Moody Publishers, 2007).

2. J. Scott Duvall and J. Daniel Hays, *Grasping God's Word: A Hands-On Approach to Reading, Interpreting, and Applying the Bible*, 4th ed. (Grand Rapids: Zondervan, 2020).

3. See "Freshening Up Your Bible Study with Dr. Jim Coakley: Early On," *Mornings with Eric and Brigitte*, Moody Radio, January 19, 2022, https://www.moodyradio.org/globalassets/radio-resources/c/coakley-early-on.pdf.

4. Jane Austen, *Pride and Prejudice* (1813; repr., Mineola, NY: Dover, 1995), 1.

5. George Orwell, *1984* (New York: Signet Classics, 1950), 1.

6. Aristotle's actual line, in section 1303b of book five of *Politics*, reads "the beginning, as the proverb says, is half of the whole," but this line has been popularly simplified to "Well begun is half done."

7. See "Freshening Up Your Bible Study with Dr. Jim Coakley: Early On."

8. Ibid.

9. Ibid.

10. See Robert Alter, *The Art of Biblical Narrative*, 2nd ed. (New York: Basic Books, 2011), 66.

11. Leland Ryken, *Words of Delight: A Literary Introduction to the Bible* (Grand Rapids: Baker, 1993), 101–103.

12. "Oh, What a Beautiful Mornin'" is the opening song from Rodgers & Hammerstein's musical film *Oklahoma!* (1955) and sung by Gordon MacRae.

13. James F. Coakley, "Marriage and Music in the Early Chapters of Genesis," in *Marriage: Its Foundation, Theology, and Mission in a Changing World*, Curt Hamner et al., eds. (Chicago: Moody Publishers, 2018), 67.

14. Jennifer Betts, "Captivating Flashback Examples in Literature," YourDictionary, https://examples.yourdictionary.com/captivating-flashback-examples-in-literature.html.

15. Charles Dickens, *A Tale of Two Cities* (Philadelphia: T. B. Peterson and Brothers, 1859), 5.

16. From Plutarch, "How a Young Man Ought to Hear Poems," 399 BC.

17. See Ward Parks, "Ring Structure and Narrative Embedding in Homer and 'Beowulf,'" *Neuphilologische Mitteilungen* (1988): 237–51.

18. This website is dedicated to chronicling the use of chiasmus in modern films and lays out the chiastic structure of over twenty films, including the ones listed: https://dejareviewer.com/deja-reviews/cinematic-chiasmus/.

19. Benjamin K. Johnson and Judith E. Rosenbaum, "(Don't) Tell Me How It Ends: Spoilers, Enjoyment, and Involvement in Television and Film," *Media Psychology* 21, no. 4 (2018): 582–612.

20. Warren Carter, *Matthew: Storyteller, Interpreter, Evangelist* (Grand Rapids: Baker, 2004), 135.

21. Ibid.

22. Ibid.

23. Adapted from John Sailhamer, *Introduction to Old Testament Theology: A Canonical Approach* (Grand Rapids: Zondervan, 1995), 294–95.

24. Edward P. J. Corbett, *Classical Rhetoric for the Modern Student* (Oxford: Oxford University Press, 1965), 429.

25. John H. Sailhamer, *Introduction to Old Testament Theology: A Canonical Approach* (Grand Rapids: Zondervan, 1995), 292.

26. Adapted from ibid., 292.

27. Adapted from ibid., 293.

28. This term was coined by Robert Longacre, who applied it in his research as Bible translation consultant to grammatical or discourse features of a text (i.e., types of verb tenses used or uncommon grammatical features). This chapter will use that term to go beyond the grammatical and discourse level and apply

it when it is done by an author through the stacking up of literary devices in a given text. See his work, "Discourse Peak as Zone of Turbulence," in *Beyond the Sentence: Discourse and Sentential Form*, ed. Jessica Wirth (Ann Arbor, MI: Karoma, 1985), 83–100.

29. Benjamin J. Noonan, "The Patriarchs' Altar-Building as Anticipation of the Israelite Conquest," in *For Us, but Not to Us: Essays on Creation, Covenant, and Context in Honor of John H. Walton*, Adam E. Miglio et al., eds. (Eugene, OR: Pickwick, 2020), 270.

30. Grant R. Osborne, *The Hermeneutical Spiral: A Comprehensive Introduction to Biblical Interpretation*, 2nd ed. (Downers Grove, IL: InterVarsity Press, 2006).

31. Ibid., 22.

32. Christopher R. Smith, *The Beauty Behind the Mask: Rediscovering the Books of the Bible* (Toronto: Clements Publishing, 2007), 14–15.

33. See Eugene H. Merrill, *Kingdom of Priests: A History of Old Testament Israel* (Grand Rapids: Baker, 2008), chapter 5.